Nutritional Fitness and Resilien

A Review of Relevant Constructs, Measures, and Links to Well-Being

Karen R. Flórez, Regina A. Shih, Margret T. Martin

RAND Project AIR FORCE

Prepared for the United States Air Force
Approved for public release; distribution unlimited

For more information on this publication, visit www.rand.org/t/RR105

Library of Congress Control Number: 2014952042
ISBN: 978-0-8330-8260-2

Support RAND

Make a tax-deductible charitable contribution at
www.rand.org/giving/contribute

www.rand.org

Preface

U.S. military personnel have been engaged in operations in Central Asia and the Middle East for the past decade. Members of the armed forces also deploy to other regions of the world. Many aspects of deployments have the potential to contribute to individual stress, such as uncertainty about deployment time lines; culture shock in theater; fear of or confrontation with death or physical injury; environmental challenges, such as extreme climates and geographical features; austere living conditions; separation from friends and family members; and reintegration after deployment. Service members and their families also manage other military-related stressors, such as frequent relocations, long work hours, and the additional family separations associated with unaccompanied tours and domestic training exercises. Some service members and their families may cope well or even thrive as they overcome adversity and accomplish challenging tasks. However, some may suffer negative consequences as a result of military-related stressors, such as physical injury, including traumatic brain injury; depression, anxiety, or other mood disorders; posttraumatic stress disorder; spiritual crises; substance abuse; family dysfunction; marital problems and dissolutions; social isolation; and in extreme cases, even suicide or suicide attempts. With the aim of preventing such deleterious outcomes rather than simply responding to them, the study of resilience is of paramount importance.

The Air Force offices of Airman and Family Services (AF/A1S), the Surgeon General (AF/SG), and the Secretary of the Air Force, Force Management and Personnel (SAF/MRM) asked the RAND Corporation to help the Air Force develop its programs to promote resiliency among military and civilian Air Force personnel and their families. This report is one in a series of nine reports that resulted from that research effort.

The overarching report, *Airman and Family Resilience: Lessons from the Scientific Literature* (Meadows and Miller, forthcoming), provides an introduction to resilience concepts and research, documents established and emerging Air Force resiliency efforts, and reviews Air Force metrics for tracking the resiliency of Air Force personnel and their families. It also provides recommendations to support the development of resilience initiatives across the Air Force. We use the term *resilience* to refer to the ability to withstand, recover from, and grow in the face of stressors and fitness, which is related, as a "state of adaptation in balance with the conditions at hand" (Mullen, 2010).

Accompanying that overarching report are eight supplemental reports that outline the constructs, metrics, and influential factors relevant to resiliency across the eight domains of Total Force Fitness:

- medical

- nutritional
- environmental
- physical
- social
- spiritual
- behavioral
- psychological.

These supplemental reports are not intended to be a comprehensive review of the entire literature within a domain. Rather, they focus on studies that consider the stress-buffering aspects of each domain, regardless of whether the term *resilience* is specifically used. This expanded the scope of the reviews to include a broader range of applicable studies and also allowed for terminology differences that occur across different disciplines (e.g., stress management, hardiness).

In this report, we identify key constructs relevant to nutritional fitness from the scientific literature. The report describes measures of food intake, dietary patterns, and behavior and the food environment and also provides evidence on health outcomes. Finally, it reviews potential interventions to promote nutritional fitness, from the environmental level, community or context-specific level, down to the individual level.

The results of these reports should be relevant to Air Force leaders who are tasked with monitoring and supporting the well-being of active duty, reserve, and guard Airmen and Air Force civilian employees, as well as their families. The results of our studies may also help broaden the scope of research on resilience and help Airmen and their families achieve optimal nutritional fitness.

The research described in this report was conducted within the Manpower, Personnel, and Training Program of RAND Project AIR FORCE as part of a fiscal year 2011 study titled "Program and Facility Support for Air Force Personnel and Family Resiliency."

RAND Project AIR FORCE

RAND Project AIR FORCE (PAF), a division of the RAND Corporation, is the U.S. Air Force's federally funded research and development center for studies and analyses. PAF provides the Air Force with independent analyses of policy alternatives affecting the development, employment, combat readiness, and support of current and future air, space, and cyber forces. Research is conducted in four programs: Force Modernization and Employment; Manpower, Personnel, and Training; Resource Management; and Strategy and Doctrine. The research reported here was prepared under contract FA7014-06-C-0001.

Additional information about PAF is available on our website:
http://www.rand.org/paf

Contents

Summary

U.S. military personnel face many sources of stress both from deployment (e.g., uncertain time lines, culture shock, confrontation with physical injury and death) and from other sources, including frequent relocations, long work hours, and family separations. Many service members and their families cope well and may even thrive as they overcome adversity and accomplish challenging tasks. However, others may suffer negative consequences, such as physical injury, depression, post-traumatic stress disorder, marital and other family problems, and, at the extreme, even suicide or suicide attempts. With the aim of preventing such deleterious outcomes, an understanding of resilience is of paramount importance.

The Air Force offices of Airman and Family Services (AF/A1S), the Surgeon General (AF/SG), and the Secretary of the Air Force, Force Management and Personnel (SAF/MRM) asked RAND to help the Air Force develop its programs to promote the resilience of military and civilian Air Force personnel and their families. In particular, the research sponsors asked RAND to assess the current state of resilience-related constructs and measures in the scientific literature and to report any evidence about initiatives that promote resilience across a number of domains. This report, focusing on nutritional fitness, is one in a series of nine reports resulting from this effort.

Nutritional fitness for Airmen can be defined as having the nutrients needed to facilitate not only good health and readiness but also resilience against the physical and mental stressors associated with military service. Nutritional fitness contributes to resilience by helping service members maintain a healthy weight, protecting them against diet-related diseases that affect physical and cognitive functions, and reducing their vulnerability to stress and depression. Achieving nutritional fitness can be challenging, however, and a lack of it—in the form of obesity—is the leading medical reason that applicants fail to qualify for military service.

Focus of This Report

This report provides an overview of the scientific literature related to nutritional fitness to help the Air Force target its nutrition-related intervention efforts more successfully. The report has three main goals:

- to identify existing measures developed for individual food intake
- to understand facilitators of and perceived barriers to healthful diets, including psychosocial and environmental factors

- to understand interventions available to promote nutritional fitness.

We will discuss the evidence addressing each of these issues in turn.

Food Intake

Food intake is typically measured by having individuals either (1) record their food consumption in real time or (2) report on their past food consumption through interviews and questionnaires. Real-time methods generally involve the *weighted record technique* (in which the individual weighs the food before recording the data) and the *estimated record* (in which an individual estimates the portion sizes of each individual foodstuff). Methods of estimating food intake from past consumption patterns include 24-hour recall, dietary history, and food frequency questionnaires.

The measures employed in the most widely used method, food frequency questionnaires, differ in their validity and reliability, and some may not be appropriate in measuring the food intake of members of the military services. For example, the representative samples used to measure the nutrient value of foods and the weight of typical food portions may have nutritional needs that are not consistent with those of some military members, who may, for example, experience extreme climates or atypical levels of physical exertion.

Research findings on food intake show that, as one might expect, the consumption of fruits, vegetables, whole grains, fat-free and low-fat dairy products, and seafood—along with limiting caloric intake—is associated with positive health outcomes. The evidence also shows that, to achieve the health outcomes necessary for resilience, it is crucial to consume fewer foods containing sodium (salt), saturated fats, trans-fats, cholesterol, added sugars, and refined grains.

There is increasing research on the role of nutrition in mental health. This research documents the importance of specific foods and nutrients (e.g., blueberries, Omega-3 fatty acids) on brain functioning and the role of anti-inflammatory foods in the etiology of depression and other psychological disorders. The hypothesis concerning the latter is that several of the pathways to inflammation (e.g., oxidative stress) can be sparked by specific foods and dietary patterns (Kiecolt-Glasser, 2010).

Facilitators and Perceived Barriers to a Healthy Diet

To understand *facilitators* and *perceived barriers* of food intake, the research literature has largely focused on fruit and vegetable intake, investigating a number of psychosocial factors to determine why some individuals have difficulty obtaining or maintaining a healthful diet. These factors include self-efficacy (i.e., confidence that one can consume more fruits and vegetables), social support, attitudes and intentions, knowledge, motivation, religiosity, and norms.

The research shows that individual and social factors need to work in tandem to achieve a nutritional pattern that foments physical and psychological resilience. For example, measures should not only study whether a person has the confidence that she/he can consume more fruits and vegetables but they should also examine whether she/he can do so in the face of *barriers* (e.g., lack of family or social support for healthy eating). The factors that appear most important to both adults and children are self-efficacy, social support, and attitudes toward healthy eating. However, much work is still needed to understand the role of these and other psychosocial factors, and more studies using reliable, validated measures are needed.

An individual's food intake can also be affected by environmental factors. For example, there is a growing body of evidence documenting the links between food environments, dietary behaviors, and adults' and children's body weight. One area of research has focused on the effect of supermarkets and other food outlets on diet and increased risk for obesity. Living nearer to a large grocery store or supermarket has been linked to better dietary quality as well as lower risk of obesity and other risk factors for chronic disease. Research on food environments, while growing, can benefit from better measures of food environments and more longitudinal studies

Nutrition-Related Interventions

Nutrition-related interventions take place on the environmental, the community, and the individual levels:

- *Environmental-level interventions* attempt to increase the availability of healthful foods (1) through greater access to large-scale food retail stores, farmers' markets, and community gardens; (2) by changing consumption cues in one's environment, such as the size of plates and physical positioning of food in a given environment; and (3) by employing communication campaigns focused on dietary-related messages.
- *Community-specific interventions* (also referred to as context-specific interventions) provide tools and resources to individuals that they can use to practice changes in dietary behavior in specific settings, such as work, school, and faith-based organizations.
- *Individual-level interventions* often employ behavioral counseling to spark changes in dietary patterns. A major characteristic of these interventions is the range of intensity, with some consisting of a single session and others of more than 20 sessions over two years.

Although some environmental interventions at all three levels have shown promise, more research is needed to assess which programs are most effective in improving nutritional fitness. For example, there is a dearth of research on intervention programs that attempt to increase access to nutritious food, and such research that does exist has not shown that these interventions have improved neighborhood residents' dietary behavior. Studies focused on increasing access to farmers' markets and community gardens have shown modest changes in adults' fruit and vegetable consumption but, again, there is insufficient research on the effectiveness of this type of intervention. Interventions that focus on environmental cues have employed such strategies as introducing dinnerware and utensils designed to achieve an appropriate portion size rather than teaching people the complexities of calculating portion size. This type of intervention appears to be especially promising in the school context, where environmental cues to overeat are powerful (e.g., the availability of energy-dense food in vending machines). In terms of health communication campaigns, those that focus on dietary-related messages generally fall in the middle of the efficacy continuum—that is, they are not as effective as seat-belt campaigns but are more effective than drug campaigns (Snyder, 2007).

The results from several workplace interventions are promising. However, workplace approaches are rare, generally of low intensity (e.g., emphasizing information and education), short term (six months or less), and focused on individual-level behaviors. In terms of school-based interventions, there is insufficient evidence suggesting that they work, although school-based physical education interventions have consistently improved health outcomes related to body fat and blood pressure in children and adolescents. More research is also needed on church-based interventions; evidence to date indicates that they have achieved short-term effects in the daily consumption of fruits and vegetables and on the weight of participating congregants. There were very few interventions designed to test the effect of family-level resources, such as social support.

Many low-intensity individual interventions have entailed disseminating information about healthful diet through the web or mail only, whereas others have supplemented this material with diet-related information disseminated by a health care provider (Lin et al., 2010). More intense individual interventions entailed counseling (either in person or over the phone) or various group counseling sessions (Lin et al., 2010). Overall, these interventions entailed a high degree of resources with little regard for the context in which individuals needed to make these dietary decisions. It is likely that many individual-level interventions could benefit from introducing environmental-level components.

Conclusion

The Air Force can harness the tools described in this report to increase the effectiveness of its nutrition programs in promoting resilience and preventing or mitigating stress. An important first step will be to measure facilitators and barriers at both individual and environmental levels to develop effective interventions that increase nutritional fitness. However, as the Air Force designs nutrition-related programs, it will be important to take account of the methodological limitations identified in this report and to consider research findings in the context of the special nutritional needs of the military population.

Acknowledgments

This research was sponsored by the Air Force Resilience office and was led by Mr. Brian P. Borda for a significant portion of the study period and by Air Force Surgeon General Lt Gen (Dr.) Charles B. Green, and Mr. William H. Booth, the Assistant Secretary of the Air Force for Manpower and Reserve Affairs (SAF/MRM).

We would like to thank the action officers from the sponsoring offices for their role in shaping the research agenda and providing feedback on interim and final briefings of the research findings. Those officers are Maj Kirby Bowling, our primary contact from the Air Force Resilience office; Col John Forbes and Lt Col David Dickey from the Air Force Surgeon General's office; and Linda Stephens-Jones from SAF/MRM. We also appreciate the insights and recommendations received from Ms. Eliza Nesmith while she was in the Air Force Services and from Lt Col Shawn Campbell while he served in the SAF/MRM office.

RAND's Sarah Meadows and Laura Miller led the overall research effort on resilience and provided extensive feedback on a previous draft of this manuscript. Donna White and Hosay Salam Yaqub provided valuable assistance formatting the manuscript and assembling the bibliography for publication.

We thank Dr. Scott J. Montain and Dr. Deborah Cohen for providing their thoughtful reviews of this report.

Abbreviations

AI	Adequate Intake
AIRC	American Institute for Cancer Research
BED	binge-eating disorder
BMI	body mass index
CHOW	Choose Health Options at Work
CVD	cardiovascular disease
DASH	Dietary Approaches to Stop Hypertension
DHA	docosahexaenoic acid
DHQ	Diet History Questionnaire
DINE	Develop Improved Nutrition Environment
EPA	Eicosapentaenoic acid
FFQ	food frequency questionnaire
IU	international unit
NCI	National Cancer Institute
NEAT	Nutrition Environment Tool
NEMS	Nutrition Environment Measures Survey
NEMS-R	Nutrition Environment Measures Survey–Restaurant
NEMS-S	Nutrition Environment Measures Survey–Store
PTSD	post-traumatic stress disorder
WCRF	World Cancer Research Fund

1. The Context of This Report[1]

This report is one of a series designed to support Air Force leaders in promoting resilience among Airmen, its civilian employees, and Air Force family members. The research sponsors requested that RAND assess the current resilience-related constructs and measures in the scientific literature and report any evidence of initiatives that promote resilience across a number of domains. We did not limit our search to research conducted in military settings or with military personnel, as Air Force leaders sought the potential opportunity to apply the results of these studies to a population that had not yet been addressed (i.e., Airmen). Further, many Air Force services support Air Force civilians and family members, and thus the results of civilian studies would apply to these populations.

This study adopts the Air Force definition of resilience: "the ability to withstand, recover and/or grow in the face of stressors and changing demands," which we found to encompass a range of definitions of resilience given throughout the scientific literature.[2] By focusing on resilience, the armed forces aim to expand their care to ensure the well-being of military personnel and their families through preventive measures and not just by treating members after they begin to experience negative outcomes (e.g., depression, anxiety, insomnia, substance abuse, post-traumatic stress disorder, or suicidal ideation).

Admiral Michael Mullen, Chairman of the Joint Chiefs of Staff from 2007 to 2011, outlined the concept of Total Force Fitness (TFF) in a special issue of the journal *Military Medicine*: "A total force that has achieved total fitness is healthy, ready, and resilient; capable of meeting challenges and surviving threats" (Mullen, 2010, p. 1). This notion of "fitness" is directly related to the concept of resilience. The same issue of *Military Medicine* also reflected the collective effort of scholars, health professionals, and military personnel, who outlined eight domains of TFF: medical, nutritional, environmental, physical, social, spiritual, behavioral, and psychological. This framework expands on the traditional conceptualization of resilience by looking beyond the psychological realm to also emphasize the mind-body connection and the interdependence of each of the eight domains.

The research sponsors requested that RAND adopt these eight fitness domains as the organizing framework for our literature review. We followed this general framework,

---

[1] Adapted from Meadows and Miller, forthcoming.

[2] The Air Force adopted this definition, which was developed by the Defense Centers of Excellence for Psychological Health and Traumatic Brain Injury (DCoE, 2011).

although in some cases we adapted the scope of a domain to better reflect the relevant research. Thus, this study resulted in eight reports, each focusing on resilience-related research in one of the TFF domains, but we note that not all of these domains are mutually exclusive. These eight reports define each domain and address the following interrelated topics:

- medical: preventive care, the presence and management of injuries, chronic conditions, and barriers and bridges to accessing appropriate quality health care (Shih, Meadows, and Martin, 2013)
- nutritional: food intake, dietary patterns and behavior, and the food environment (Flórez, Shih, and Martin, 2014)
- environmental: environmental stressors and potential workplace injuries and preventive and protective factors (Shih, Meadows, Mendeloff, and Bowling, forthcoming)
- physical: physical activity and fitness (Robson, 2013)
- social: social fitness and social support from family, friends, coworkers/unit members, neighbors, and cyber communities (McGene, 2013)
- spiritual: spiritual worldview, personal religious or spiritual practices and rituals, support from a spiritual community, and spiritual coping (Yeung and Martin, 2013)
- behavioral: health behaviors related to sleep and to drug, alcohol, and tobacco use (Robson and Salcedo, forthcoming)
- psychological: self-regulation, positive and negative affect, perceived control, self-efficacy, self-esteem, optimism, adaptability, self-awareness, and emotional intelligence (Robson, 2014).

These reports are not intended to be comprehensive reviews of the entire literature within a domain. Rather, they focus on those studies that consider the stress-buffering aspects of each domain, regardless of whether the term *resilience* is specifically used. This expanded the scope of the reviews to include a broader range of studies and also allowed for differences in the terminology used across different disciplines (e.g., stress management, hardiness). We sought evidence both on the main effects of resilience factors in each domain (i.e., those that promote general well-being) and on the indirect or interactive effects (i.e., those that buffer the negative effects of stress).

Because the Air Force commissioned this research to specifically address individuals' capacity to be resilient, and thus their well-being, our reports do not address whether or how fitness in each of the eight TFF domains could be linked to other outcomes of interest to the military, such as performance, military discipline, unit readiness, personnel costs, attrition, or retention. Those worthy topics were beyond the scope of this project.

Some other important parameters shaped this literature review. First, across the study, we focused on research from the past decade, although older studies are included, particularly landmark studies that still define the research landscape or where a particular line of inquiry has been dormant in recent years. Second, we prioritized research on adults in the United States. Research on children was included where particularly germane (e.g., in discussions of family as a form of social support), and, occasionally, research on adults in other Western nations is referenced or subsumed within a large study. Research on elderly populations was generally excluded. Third, we prioritized literature reviews, meta-analyses, and on-going bodies of research over more singular smaller-scale studies.

The search for evidence on ways to promote resilience in each domain included both actions that individuals could take as well as actions that organizations could take, such as information campaigns, policies, directives, programs, initiatives, facilities, or other resources. We did not filter out evidence related to Air Force practices already under way, as the Air Force was interested both in research related to existing practices and in research that might suggest new paths for promoting resilience. Our aim was not to collect examples of creative or promising initiatives at large but to seek scholarly publications assessing the stress-buffering capacity of initiatives. Thus, in general, this collection of reviews does not address initiatives that have not yet been evaluated for their effect.

Building on the foundation of the eight reports that assess the scientific literature in each domain, RAND prepared an overarching report that brings together the highlights of these reviews and examines their relevance to current Air Force metrics and programs. That ninth report, *Airman and Family Resilience: Lessons from the Scientific Literature,* provides a more in-depth introduction to resilience concepts and research, presents our model of the relationship between resilience and TFF, documents established and emerging Air Force resiliency efforts, and reviews the Air Force metrics for tracking the resiliency of Air Force personnel and their families. By comparing the information we found in the research literature to Air Force practices, we were able to provide recommendations to support the development of initiatives to promote resilience across the Air Force. Although the overview report contains Air Force–specific recommendations that take into account all eight domains and existing Air Force practices, some are applicable to the military more generally and are highlighted at the end of this report.

2. Background to This Report

This report focuses on nutritional fitness. Nutritional fitness for Airmen can be defined as having the nutrients needed to facilitate not only good health and readiness but also resilience against the physical and mental stressors associated with military service. Nutritional fitness contributes to resilience by helping service members maintain a healthy weight, protecting them against diet-related diseases that affect physical and cognitive function, and reducing their vulnerability to stress and depression. Achieving nutritional fitness can be challenging, however, and a lack of it—in the form of obesity— is the leading medical reason that applicants fail to qualify for military service.

Achieving nutritional fitness begins with access to high-quality foodstuffs that can provide a sufficient amount of nutrients needed to withstand the physical and mental challenges associated with military service. Proper nutrition is known to facilitate physical resilience during service, both during deployments and at home, and to protect against diet-related diseases throughout the life course. Nutrition also appears to directly affect mental health outcomes (e.g., certain food combinations rich in antioxidant vitamins reduced the risk of Alzheimer disease), including stress and depression. Therefore, nutrition can directly enhance resilience.

However, achieving a healthful diet involves multiple and complex factors that can make individual consumption of adequate amount of micro- and macronutrients difficult. In the United States, for example, more than one-third of adults (35.7 percent) are obese (Ogden et al., 2012) yet also undernourished in several key nutrients, such as fiber and calcium. Similarly, obesity is becoming a major public health issue among military populations (Montain, Carvey, and Stephens, 2010). For example, only one in four young adults ages 17–24 is eligible for military service, and being overweight or obese is the leading medical reason why applicants fail to qualify for service (Mission: Readiness Report, 2010).

We know that reducing caloric consumption is the most important factor in obesity control, but improving diet quality, encouraging healthy food choices, and meeting specific nutritional requirements are also key factors in curtailing a variety of chronic diseases. For example, the Dietary Guidelines for Americans emphasize three major goals for Americans (Dietary Guidelines Advisory Committee, 2010):

- Balance calories with physical activity to manage weight.
- Consume more of certain foods and nutrients such as fruits, vegetables, whole grains, fat-free and low-fat dairy products, and seafood, while also limited caloric intake.

- Consume fewer foods with sodium (salt), saturated fats, trans-fats, cholesterol, added sugars, and refined grains.

Meeting these goals at the individual level presents a major challenge, given that, on average, Americans of all ages consume too few vegetables, fruits, high-fiber whole grains, low-fat milk and milk products, and seafood, and they eat too much added sugars, solid fats, refined grains, and sodium. Added sugars and solid fats contribute approximately 35 percent of calories to the American diet.

Understanding which diet-related factors are most relevant for resilience involves measuring a variety of components that constitute a healthy diet. Specifically, it involves measuring food intake at the individual level; understanding facilitators and perceived barriers to healthy eating, including psychosocial and environmental factors; and understanding available interventions designed to promote nutritional fitness. However, the metrics associated with some of these concepts vary widely in their quality, hampering their applicability to the military and civilian context alike. One consequence of these measurement issues is inconsistency across studies that focus on the association of nutrition concepts and diet-related outcomes.

Focus of This Report

This report aims to provide a thorough overview of the scientific literature related to nutritional fitness to help the Air Force target its nutrition-related intervention efforts more successfully. The report has three main goals:

- to identify existing measures developed for individual food intake
- to understand facilitators of and perceived barriers to healthful diets, including psychosocial and environmental factors
- to understand interventions available to promote nutritional fitness.

Organization of This Report

The remainder of this report consists of three chapters:

- In Chapter Three, we examine existing measures of individual food intake and what is known about the relationship between food intake and health outcomes.
- In Chapter Four, we examine psychosocial and environmental facilitators of and perceived barriers to healthful diets.
- In Chapter Five, we examine interventions available to promote nutritional fitness.
- Chapter Six presents our conclusions.

3. Nutritional Fitness Constructs, Measures, and Links to Health Outcomes

"The wise man should consider that health is the greatest of human blessings. Let food be your medicine."

— Hippocrates, Physician

Measuring food intake at the individual level is crucial in determining the associations between diet and resilience. In this chapter, we begin our examination of nutritional fitness constructs by focusing on measures of food intake and their links to health outcomes. We describe existing measures of food intake and discuss the strengths and challenges associated with those methods. Then we discuss what is known about health outcomes associated with food intake.

Measures of Food Intake

Food intake can be estimated *at the time of eating* or *from past eating patterns* (Van Staveren and Ocké, 2006):

- **Real-time measures.** The most widely used real-time methods are the *weighted record technique* and the *estimated record*. The former requires that the individual weigh food and record the data later, whereas the latter requires that an individual estimate the portion sizes of each foodstuff (Van Staveren and Ocké, 2006).
- **Estimates of past consumption.** The three most-common methods for estimating food intake from past consumption patterns are *24-hour recall*, *dietary history*, and *food frequency questionnaires*. All three methods involve interviewing individuals about foods consumed; however, dietary history and food frequency methods focus on habitual diet, whereas 24-hour recall focuses on one's current diet.

Food Frequency Questionnaires

The most widely used approach for estimating past consumption is the food frequency questionnaire (FFQ) method, which involves the administration of questionnaires to assess individuals' consumption of specific foods. The food to be measured is derived from a list that is preselected by the researchers, and some FFQs also ask the portion size for each food item. Responses from questionnaires can be converted into daily nutrient intake estimates and analyzed.

Block Food Frequency Questionnaire. Most food frequency studies use modified versions of the Block FFQ (Block et al., 1990; Mares-Perlman et al., 1993) and the Willet FFQ (Willett and Lenart, 1998). However, the latter does not specifically ask about portion sizes, which has resulted in lower validity and reliability than in the Block FFQ (Subar et al., 2001). The Block FFQ asks about 106 foods and their respective portion sizes, and the information is based on national dietary data (Block et al., 1990; Mares-Perlman et al., 1993). The Block FFQ can also be adapted by adding/subtracting appropriate foods for a particular population (e.g., African Americans, Latinos) (Carithers et al., 2009; Nath and Huffman, 2005). However, some issues have been identified when using the Block FFQ, such as comprehension, order of food items, and intake of seasonal foods (Subar et al., 2001).

Diet History Questionnaire. The National Cancer Institute (NCI) (2013b) has addressed the issues in the Block FFQ and created a diet history questionnaire (DHQ) (Subar et al., 2001). This questionnaire consists of 124 food items and includes questions about both portion size and dietary supplement. It takes about one hour to complete and has very high response rate despite the length of the instrument. A machine-readable paper-and-pencil version can be scanned and analyzed. There is also a web-based version called the DHQ*Web. The advantage of the latter is that it can be easily analyzed with the Diet*Cal software developed by NCI. A new version of the DHQ (i.e., DHQ II), the DHQ*Web, Diet*Cal software and all other pertinent details are available at National Cancer Institute (2013a)

Methodological Challenges Associated with FFQs. Despite their usefulness, FFQs may not always be the most appropriate approach to measure food intake. For example, FFQs may not have the level of detail needed for intervention studies that seek to detect very subtle differences in dietary changes. Moreover, the databases used to measure foods, their nutrient values, and weights for typical food portions derive from the dietary intake component of the National Health and Nutrition Examination Survey (U.S. Department of Agriculture, 2013). Given that these data are derived from a nationally representative sample, some caution is warranted when extrapolating these guidelines to individuals in extreme climates or to persons with atypical levels of physical exertion. The American Dietetic Association has developed useful nutrient and fluid intake guidelines for competitive athletes and those in extreme climates (Rodriguez, Di Marco, and Langley, 2009); however, there are no food intake instruments based on these guidelines. Other important issues to take heed of when using FFQs are the following:

- Different study designs (e.g., case-control, cross-sectional) involve modifications in the way food-frequency data are collected. For example, an FFQ for use in a retrospective case–control study should reflect dietary consumption at the relevant time points.
- The food items listed in an FFQ need to be culturally appropriate for the target population. This will ensure a reduction in systematic error produced by the lack of relevancy a particular foodstuff may have for a given population.
- Modification of an existing questionnaire needs to be validated even if prior validation of the original instrument has been carried out.
- Last, the usefulness of any method for assessing food intake will vary according to the purpose. For example, large epidemiological studies need to employ methods that can yield useful data on habitual diet while minimizing respondent burden.

Research Using Dietary Biomarkers

To address this issue of bias, another approach for measuring food intake is to use dietary biomarkers, such as doubly labeled water (often used for metabolic rate and total energy expenditure) or urinary total nitrogen/potassium (used to measure total daily protein consumption and potassium intake) (Jenab et al., 2009). Also, predictive dietary biomarkers, such as urinary sucrose or fructose, and concentration/replacement dietary biomarkers are used to estimate diet-disease risk associations (e.g., individual fatty acids). Although the use of biomarkers has advantages over self-reported measures of food intake, employing biochemical techniques is expensive and invasive, and only a single nutrient can be assessed at a given time (Cade et al., 2002). Further, biomarkers may not directly measure intake, since error may be introduced by an array of factors (e.g., a person's metabolism, excretion, and homeostatic mechanisms). In the few studies examining the correlation between dietary reference method and biomarkers, there were no substantial differences in measurement error in relation to energy, fat, vitamin C, or vitamin A (Cade et al., 2002). Therefore, it is difficult to categorize this or any other method as the gold standard, given that all techniques are associated with specific sources of errors.

Health Outcomes Associated with Food Intake

The majority of research on individuals' food intake focuses on the high calorie foods and beverages in the American diet. According to recent estimates, breads, cookies, and donuts are the top source of calories for American adults (Dietary Guidelines Advisory Committee, 2010. Pizza was ranked as the second source of calorie intake for children, and soda/energy/sports drinks were ranked third (Dietary Guidelines Advisory Committee, 2010). The immediate implication of this kind of energy-dense diet (i.e., a diet high in calories) is increased difficulty in "burning" these calories through normal body functions, thus producing the calorie imbalance associated with weight gain. For example, evidence suggests that certain dietary factors are independently associated with long-term weight gain in women and men in the United States (Mozaffarian et al., 2011). Specifically, the four-year weight gain associated with potato chips was 1.69 pounds, potatoes 1.28 pounds, sugar-sweetened beverages 1.00 pounds, unprocessed red meats 0.95 pounds, and processed meats 0.93 pounds (Mozaffarian et al., 2011).

The association between energy-dense diets and overweight and obesity is also consistently strong across different segments of the population (e.g., children, adolescents). Increasingly, obesity is associated with a variety of health outcomes, most notably certain cancers (e.g., colon), cardiovascular disease (CVD), and diabetes. Less research has been conducted on the effect of obesity on psychological outcomes, but research suggests an association between adult obesity and critical factors required for optimal mental health (e.g., reduction in white and gray-matter brain volume, reduction in cognitive functioning) (Walsh, 2011).[3]

There is a growing body of research on the role of nutrition in mental health. One line of research documents the importance of specific foods and nutrients (e.g., blueberries, Omega-3 fatty acids) on brain functioning (e.g., cognitive processes, emotions) (Gómez-Pinilla, 2008). Another significant line of research highlights the role of anti-inflammatory foods in the etiology of depression and other psychological disorders (Kiecolt-Glasser, 2010). The focus is on inflammation because the latter is the common link among the leading causes of death (e.g., diabetes, CVD) as well as depression (Kiecolt-Glasser, 2010). The hypothesis is that several of the pathways to inflammation (e.g., oxidative stress) can be sparked by specific foods and dietary patterns (Kiecolt-Glasser, 2010).

In this chapter, we describe findings from the body of research on physical and mental health associated with individuals' consumption of macronutrients; micronutrients; water, alcohol, and other beverages; and dietary supplements. We also discuss what is known about health outcomes associated with broader dietary patterns and behavior.

Macronutrients

In this section, we discuss scientific findings related to four types of macronutrients: carbohydrates, protein, fat, and dairy products.

Carbohydrates. Carbohydrates (i.e., sugars, starches, fibers) are one of the primary macronutrients (i.e., the dietary components that provide bulk energy) (National Institutes of Medicine, 2005).

In the scientific literature, there is some consistency in the findings regarding fiber, whole grains and fruits and vegetables and obesity and obesity-related health outcomes. For example, dietary fiber has been consistently associated with lower body weight (Slavin, 2008), and whole grain intake (e.g., cereal fibers) has been shown to have protective effects against CVD (Dietary Guidelines Advisory Committee , 2010).

There is also strong evidence regarding overall intake of fruits and vegetables in their protective effects against cancer of the mouth, pharynx, larynx, and esophagus, at least among the highest consumers of vegetables and fruits (World Cancer Research Fund and American Institute for Cancer Research, [WCRF/AIRC] 2007). Some studies have found that certain vegetables have direct protective effects (e.g., carrots), and others have found that raw vegetables have a protective effect against esophageal cancer (WCRF/AIRC, 2007). Micronutrients found in vegetables and fruits (e.g., beta carotene and lycopene, folate, vitamin C, vitamin D, vitamin E) are hypothesized to be the mechanisms by which vegetables and fruits exert their protective effect against certain cancers (WCRF/AIRC, 2007).

---

[3] Obesity is discussed further in the companion report on the medical fitness domain.

In the United States, there is modest evidence documenting an inverse relationship between vegetable/fruit consumption and myocardial infarction and stroke, with significantly larger, positive effects documented above five servings of vegetables and fruits per day (Genkinger et al., 2004; Hung et al., 2004; Joshipura et al., 2009; Tucker et al., 2005). There is also modest evidence that consumption of fruit and vegetables is inversely associated with blood pressure (Wang et al., 2008), cholesterol in international samples (Kelley, Kelley, and Franklin, 2006; Mirmiran et al., 2009; Radhika et al., 2008), body weight with samples from different countries (Bes-Rastrollo et al., 2006; Buijsse et al., 2009; Davis, Hodges, and Gillham, 2006; Fujikoka et a., 2006; Goss and Grubbs, 2005; He et al., 2004; Ortega et al., 2006; Radhika et al., 2008; Tanumihardjo et al., 2009; Vioque et al., 2008; Xu, Yin, and Tong, 2007).

There is mixed evidence regarding the effects of carbohydrates on other diet-related diseases. These include the association between dietary fiber and type 2 diabetes as well as some gastrointestinal diseases (Slavin, 2008). Further research is needed to elucidate the relationship between type 2 diabetes and fruit and vegetable intake. For example, some research indicates a protective effect from vegetables and not fruit, from some vegetables more than others (e.g., direct association with potato- but not tomato-based products), and from overall consumption of fruits and vegetables rather than specific foodstuffs (Liu et al., 2004; Halton, 2006b; Wang et al., 2006). The weight of the evidence in the area of sugar-sweetened beverages and energy intake and body weight is more consistent. A fair amount of research has found an association between sugar-sweetened beverages and increased body weight in adults; however, studies have found no association between obesity risk and sugar intake (Sun and Empie, 2007).

An important focus of the literature on carbohydrates concerns their role in weight reduction. Popularized by diets such as Atkins and the Zone Diet, the idea proliferated that carbohydrates could be the main contributor to weight gain. Specifically, the developers of these diets claimed that certain carbohydrates could negatively affect weight by spiking blood glucose levels that would produce feelings of intense hunger. Other health outcomes said to be affected by these types of carbohydrates were type 2 diabetes and metabolic syndrome. These diets used the glycemic index to categorize carbohydrates by their effects on blood glucose levels, and the glycemic load was the score based on portion size. The diets recommended limited or no consumption of some fruits, vegetables, and grains. For example, bananas have a glycemic load of 13 and the average serving of potato chips has a glycemic load of 11.

Despite the popularity of these diets, most research shows no difference between high-glycemic-index and low-glycemic-index diets on weight or weight loss. According to the Dietary Guidelines Advisory 2010), five of seven randomized controlled trials (Philippou et al., 2009; Pittas et al., 2006; Raatz et al., 2005; Sichieri et al., 2007; Sloth et al., 2004; Abete, Parra, and Martinez, 2008; de Rougemont et al., 2007), both prospective cohort studies (Deierlein, Siega-Riz, and Herring, 2008; Hare-Bruun, Flint, and Heitmann, 2006), and six of seven cross-sectional studies showed no association between glycemic index or load and weight or body mass index (BMI) (Hui and Nelson, 2006; Lau et al., 2006; Liese et al., 2005; Mendez et al.,

2009; Milton et al., 2007; Nielsen et al., 2005; Murakami et al., 2007). Further, there is inconsistent evidence of an association between high glycemic index and type 2 diabetes (i.e., five yes, four no, and one inverse) (Barclay et al., 2007; Halton et al., 2006; Hodge et al., 2004; Krishnan et al., 2007; Mosdøl et al., 2007; Sahyoun et al., 2008; Schulz et al., 2006; Schulze et al., 2004; Stevens et al., 2002; Villegas et al., 2007). Consuming low-GI carbohydrates (that is, low in the glycemic index) before exercise has not been found to affect performance despite popular recommendations (Donaldson, Perry, and Rose, 2010).

Other highlights from the Dietary Guidelines Advisory Committee (2010) and recent reviews in the literature include the following:

- There is limited evidence that increased intake of vegetables and/or fruits protects both children and adults against weight gain (BMI).
- "100 percent fruit juice" has not been associated with body weight, but limited evidence has linked 100 percent juice with higher BMI among children/adolescents who are overweight and obese.
- Intake of at least two and one-half cups of vegetables and fruits per day is associated with reduced risk of CVD, including heart attack and stroke.
- There is moderate evidence to show that adults who eat whole grains that are high in fiber have lower weight than adults who do not eat as much high-fiber grains.
- Diets that comprise multicolored fruits and vegetables (a "rainbow diet") are beneficial because they may prevent and ameliorate psychopathologies (Gómez-Pinilla, 2008; Walsh, 2011). This is likely a result of the anti-inflammatory properties in many vegetables (Kiecolt-Glaser, 2010).

Last, added sugar (i.e., not the sugar naturally occurring in food such as fruits and vegetables) has been found to have two major health implications. First, added sugars are a major barrier to maintaining proper calorie balance. Sugar is high in calories, is often consumed in conjunction with other dense nutrients, such as fat and refined grains (e.g., cakes, doughnuts), and can easily be overconsumed (Dietary Guidelines Advisory Committee, 2010). The research on added sugar, which has mainly focused on sugar-sweetened beverages, has yielded the following results:

- Strong evidence shows that children and adolescents who consume more sugar-sweetened beverages have higher BMI than those who do not.
- Moderate evidence indicates that adults who consume more sugar-sweetened beverages have higher BMI than those who do not.
- Added sugars are strongly associated with an increase in the risk of dental caries (i.e., cavities).

Second, added sugars have been found to negatively affect the molecules related to cellular energy control that are at the crux of various neurodegenerative diseases, such as Alzheimer's (Gómez-Pinilla, 2011). For example, animal studies show a significant decline in rats' scores of the spatial learning matter maze test when they had been fed a "junk" type diet (i.e., diets high in refined sugars and saturated fats). However, further research in humans is needed to establish the association between added sugars and neuronal health.

Protein. Protein is an essential component of adequate nutrition; however, protein intake in the United States exceeds the amounts recommended by the Dietary Guidelines Advisory Committee. Specifically, the recommendation is 46 grams per day for women ages 19–70 and 56 grams for men, but current consumption is 70.1 grams for women and 101.9 grams for men (Moshfegh et al., 2009). Further, a salient feature of this overconsumption is that protein is largely high-fat and animal-based, and some research points to the negative effects of animal protein on cancer, CVD, blood pressure, hypertension, and body weight (Dietary Guidelines Advisory, 2010).

However, the strength of the association between animal protein and health outcomes varies widely. For example, there is strong evidence supporting the link between red meats and processed meats to colorectal cancer (WCRF/AICR, 2007); however, research investigating the effect of animal protein on CVD and blood pressure is less clear (Dietary Guidelines Advisory Committee, 2010).

There is also increasing interest in the role of protein in weight loss. Spearheaded by the low-carbohydrate diet movement, increased consumption of protein (especially animal-based protein) in conjunction with decreased consumption of carbohydrates was believed by many to be an effective method for weight loss and weight control. However, there is no evidence to suggest that high-protein/low-carbohydrate diets are more effective than diets that place less emphasis on protein on long-term (i.e., more than six months) weight loss (Avenell et al., 2004; Dale et al., 2009; Due et al., 2008; Frisch et al., 2009; McAuley et al., 2005; Nordmann et al., 2006; Sacks et al., 2009; Tay et al., 2008), although one well-designed randomized controlled trial did show high-protein diets (e.g., Atkins diet) to be more effective than other diets among premenopausal, overweight, and obese women (Gardner et al., 2007). Further, high-protein diets have been linked to worsening of mood, increasing fatigue, dizziness, irritability, headaches, confusion, and sleep problems (Lloyd, Green, and Rogers, 1994; Wells and Read, 1996; Butki, Baumstark, and Driver, 2003). High protein consumption has been shown to increase women's risk of developing severely depressed mood but it did have a protective effect on men (Wolfe et al., 2011).

There is some evidence on the differential effects on weight of animal-based protein relative to plant-based protein. Although limited, research suggests that a vegetarian or vegan diet may confer some benefits on weight loss. Specifically, vegetarians and vegans consistently have lower BMIs than non-vegetarians (Spencer et al., 2003; Craig, 2009). However, given the weaker design of studies investigating the role of vegetarian and vegan diets on weight loss, more research is needed to understand the role of protein, whether animal-based or plant-based, on weight loss and healthy weight maintenance.

The Dietary Guidelines Advisory Committee cites tree nuts (i.e., walnuts, almonds, and pistachios) and seafood as good sources of protein. This is based on the moderate evidence that peanuts and other nuts reduce the risk of CVD when consumed as part of a diet that is within the caloric needs of an individual. There is also moderate evidence of the benefits of consuming certain types of seafood (e.g., reduced cardiac deaths among individuals without pre-existing CVD). Specifically, there is strong evidence suggesting that fatty fish rich in Omega-3 fatty acids (e.g., salmon, tuna) confer these health benefits. The guidelines stipulate that consuming eight ounces of seafood per week provides an adequate amount of eicosapentaenoic acid (EPA) and docosahexaenoic acid (DHA) and protects against the overconsumption of methyl mercury. The latter can be found in seafood, but if a variety of seafood high in EPA and DHA amounts is consumed in moderation, the risks posed by methyl mercury are minimal.

Fat. The Dietary Guidelines Advisory Committee recommends replacing saturated fat with monounsaturated and polyunsaturated fatty acids as well as limiting total fat to 30–40 percent of total energy and limiting saturated fats to 10 percent of fat intake. Some other recommendations for fat intake are rather vague (e.g., reduce the intake of calories from fat, limit the consumption of foods containing solid fats). We highlight some other findings from the Dietary Guidelines Advisory Committee (U.S. Department of Agriculture and U.S. Department of Health and Human Services, 2010) and other pertinent literature regarding fat and health:

- Strong evidence suggests that saturated fatty acids should not be consumed in great quantities; they are linked to higher levels of blood total cholesterol and low-density lipoprotein.
- Trans fatty acids have been associated with increased risk for CVD.
- A moderate amount of, but consistent, research has found an association between meat consumption (especially red meat) and an increased risk of diabetes, CVD, and certain cancers (U.S. Department of Agriculture and U.S. Department of Health and Human Services, 2010). Further, a recent study found an increased risk in mortality for those consuming one serving per day of unprocessed red meat (Hazard Ratio 1.13 [1.07–1.20]) and of processed red meat (Hazard Ratio 1.20 [1.15–1.24]) and found that substituting one serving per day of other foods (e.g., fish) for one serving per day of red meat was associated with a 7–19 percent lower mortality risk (Pan et al., 2012).
- Animal research shows that diets high in saturated fat can spark a decline in cognitive functioning and aggravate cognitive impairment after brain trauma in rodents (Gómez-Pinilla, 2008).
- Saturated fat has been associated with cognitive decline in aging populations (Gómez-Pinilla, 2008).

Dairy. Dairy is high in calcium, a micronutrient essential for optimal bone health (U.S. Department of Health and Human Services, 2004). The recommended amounts of dairy are three cups per day of fat-free or low-fat milk or milk products for adults and children and adolescents ages 9–18, two and one-half cups per day for children ages 4–8 years, and two cups for children ages 2–3 years. However, some individuals have trouble digesting the lactose found in dairy and others do not consume dairy at all (e.g., vegans). Those who are lactose-intolerant can choose from a variety of lactose-reduced foods that contain adequate amounts of calcium (U.S. Department of Health and Human Services, 2004). There is also a wide variety of non-dairy calcium-rich foods, such as green leafy vegetables, beans/legumes, and nuts (see National Institutes of Health, 2012).

Dairy has also been linked to certain health outcomes: A moderate amount of research shows that low-fat dairy reduces the risk of CVD and type 2 diabetes and may lower blood pressure in adults (Dietary Guidelines Advisory Committee, 2010). Some research suggests that consumption of dairy products protects children and adults from weight gain, but there are some inconsistent findings (Louie et al., 2011). However, excessive intake of dietary lipids and dairy consumption has been shown to increase the risk of Parkinson's disease (Sadiq-Butt and Sultan, 2011; Chen et al., 2007).

Micronutrients

Micronutrients are specific nutrients (e.g., vitamin C) that enable the body to produce enzymes, hormones, and other substances essential for proper growth and development (Centers for Disease Control and Prevention, 2011. The necessary amount of micronutrients needed for optimal health is quite complex and varies widely according to populations (e.g., elderly, women). There are also stark differences in the evidence regarding micronutrients and health in that some have been systematically researched but others have not received much attention. We discuss several micronutrients below, including sodium, potassium, calcium, vitamin D, Omega-3 fatty acids, and curcumin.

Sodium. Sodium is the most widely researched micronutrient, because the U.S. population far exceeds the recommended intake of sodium, partially due to the overconsumption of processed foods.

Decreased sodium intake has been strongly associated with a drop in blood pressure, especially among populations at risk for chronic diseases (e.g., African Americans, persons older than 51) as well as other vulnerable populations (e.g., children). The current recommendation is to keep daily sodium intake to less than 2,300 milligrams (mg) and 1,500 (mg) for vulnerable populations. However, only 15 percent of Americans adhere to these recommendations. Physically active individuals may need to modestly *increase* their intake over these recommended amounts to replace sodium lost in sweat (National Institutes of Medicine, 2004).

Other Micronutrients. Other well-researched micronutrients have been associated with the following health conditions:

- **Potassium:** Moderate potassium deficiency (i.e., not hypokalemia or the condition that occurs when potassium levels are below 35 mEq/L) is associated with increased risk of developing kidney stones and bone loss.
- **Calcium**: Calcium is associated with preservation of bone density and is crucial in nerve transmission, constriction and dilation of blood vessels, and muscle contraction.
- **Vitamin D**: A growing number of studies link vitamin D to decreased risk of injury and improved training and performance in athletes (Larson-Meyer and Willis, 2010). Several studies suggest associations between vitamin D deficiency and cognitive impairment, depression, bipolar disorder, and schizophrenia (Walsh, 2011). Vitamin D deficiency

15

results in rickets in children and osteomalacia (i.e., softening of the bones) in adults. Recommended amounts of vitamin D are 600 international units (IU) (15 mcg) per day for children and most adults and 800 IU (20 mcg) for adults older than 70 years. The most common source of exposure to vitamin D is from the ultraviolet rays in sunlight, although it can also be obtained from food (e.g., the flesh of fatty fish, egg yolks, some mushrooms) (National Institutes of Health, 2011).

- **Omega-3 fatty acids**: Omega-3 fatty acids are found naturally in fish (salmon), kiwi fruit, butternuts, and walnuts but can also be consumed in supplement form (e.g., fish oil). The strongest link between Omega-3 fatty acids and health is with CVD. Fatty fish, such as salmon, mackerel, herring, lake trout, sardines, and albacore tuna, are high in Omega-3 fatty acids (American Heart Association, 2010). The American Heart Association recommends eating fish (particularly fatty fish) at least two times (two servings) a week, each serving being 3.5 ounces of cooked fish or about three-quarters of a cup of flaked fish. Some observational studies have found that increased consumption of fish oils rich in Omega-3 long-chain polyunsaturated fatty acids (Omega-3) may reduce the chance of developing dementia, and other studies show no effect (Sydenham, Dangour, and Lim, 2012).
- **Curcumin**: This is the primary component of the turmeric plant, which is often used as a spice in traditional Southeast Asian cuisine (e.g., curry). Curcumin has been shown to counteract neuronal dysfunction in humans and animals and is also is associated with reversal of certain pathologies involved in rats with traumatic brain injuries (Gómez-Pinilla, 2011). However, more studies are needed before specific dietary recommendations can be made.

Water, Alcohol, Energy Drinks, and Other Beverages

In this section, we consider what is known about the consumption of water, alcohol, energy drinks, and other beverages.

Water. Although the consumption of water has been established as a crucial component of a healthy diet, establishing recommended amounts is rather complex. Indeed, the National Institutes of Medicine have not generated concrete recommendations for civilian populations, since evidence suggests that Americans tend to consume adequate amounts of water directly or through water contained in such foodstuffs as fruits and vegetables. However, because heat and physical activity have a tremendous effect on the maintenance of adequate water levels, especially during heat waves or physical exertion, people should be particularly careful to maintain adequate water intake.

Studies on the role of water and physical activity in athletes and the military service members have shown that a lack of water consumption can lead to a decrease in physical performance, such as reduced endurance and increased fatigue. Studies on physical activity executed in hot temperatures has demonstrated strong associations between dehydration and hyperthermia, reduced stroke volume and cardiac output, decrease in blood pressure, and reduced blow flow to muscles (Popkin, D'anci, and Rosenberg, 2010). Further, dehydration has been shown to affect mood and cognitive functioning (e.g., concentration, alertness), although the effect is highly contingent on the level of dehydration the individual is experiencing.

Although there is strong evidence linking water to certain chronic diseases (e.g., urolithiasis), the general position of the National Institutes of Medicine is that there is insufficient evidence to establish water intake recommendations as a way to reduce the risk of chronic diseases (National Institutes of Medicine, 2005. Although adequate intake) levels have been set according to age and gender, some argue that these estimates are riddled with measurement issues given the myriad of variables that can affect intake (e.g., the environment, an individual's health status) (Popkin, D'anci, and Rosenberg, 2010). Further research is needed to develop reliable estimates of adequate water intake.

Alcohol. Some research exists on the purported health benefits of alcohol consumption as well as the role of alcohol in diet-related disease (e.g., obesity):[4]

- There is strong evidence from observational studies that moderate drinking (i.e., consumption of up to one drink per day for women and up to two drinks per day for men) is associated with a lower risk of CVD.
- Although further research is needed, some studies suggest that moderate alcohol intake is associated with a reduced risk of all-cause mortality among middle-aged and older adults and preservation with cognitive functioning in this same population (Emberson et al., 2005; Elkind et al., 2005; Mukamal et al., 2005a, 2005b; Di Castelnuovo, 2006).
- Some studies have shown that moderate levels of drinking are not associated with weight gain among women or men (Liu et al., 1994; Sammel et al., 2003; Sherwood et al., 2000; Wannamethee and Shaper, 2003; Wannamethee et al., 2004; Koh-Banerjee et al., 2003; Tolstrup et al., 2008). Other studies do show an association between alcohol consumption and weight gain, perhaps due to the high sugar components of mixed drinks (U.S. Department of Agriculture and U.S., Department of Human Services, 2010).

Moderate levels of alcohol can confer certain health benefits on some adults, but alcohol should never be consumed by young children, pregnant women, persons taking medications that may interact with alcohol, and individuals with certain medical conditions (e.g., people with liver disease) (Dietary Guidelines Advisory Committee, 2010).

Energy Drinks. Energy drinks (e.g., Red Bull) are increasingly consumed by Americans, especially young men. Energy drinks are also the preferred caffeine-containing product among the younger military population (Montain et al., 2012). Energy drinks have been marketed quite aggressively as "performance enhancing" in the United States with little evidence that they improve physical performance (i.e., physical endurance, strength).

Of the evidence suggesting increased performance from consumption of energy drinks, most studies show that caffeine (i.e., the main component in energy drinks) is the main factor affecting

---

[4] Evidence on the deleterious effects of alcohol abuse on health is explained in the companion report on the behavioral domain.

performance. The latter has been associated with enhanced endurance among athletes and male non-athletes (Laurent et al., 2000).

Other components of energy drinks have rarely been studied and thus little is known about the effects of these ingredients in conjunction with caffeine on performance and health. We highlight here some findings from the few studies focused on components of energy drinks:

- **Taurine**: The amount of taurine found in energy drinks is far below the amount expected to deliver either therapeutic effects (e.g., some studies found taurine to have anti-inflammatory properties; others have found that it can improve exercise performance) or adverse effects (Higgins, Tuttle, and Higgins, 2010, p. 1036).
- **Guarana**: This rainforest vine is traditionally used by Amazonian peoples for energy, and it is considered a stimulant. Although energy drinks do not contain enough guarana to cause harm, some young adults have been reported to overdose on caffeine contained in drinks with guarana as an ingredient.
- **Ginseng**: This herbal supplement is thought to increase resistance to stress and fatigue; however, its performance enhancement benefits have yet to be definitively shown in scientific studies (Bahrke, Morgan, and Stegner, 2009).
- **Ginkgo biloba**: Not enough studies have been done to confirm the positive or negative effects of ginkgo biloba on humans (Nicolai et al., 2009).
- **L-carnitine**: This amino has been found to improve performance and recovery among some samples of athletes (Karlic and Lohninger, 2004).
- **Sugar:** Sugar is a key ingredient in energy drinks, given the role of glucose in the natural production of energy (Higgins, Tuttle, and Higgins, 2010). Administration of glucose before and during prolonged periods of exercise (i.e., more than an hour) has been associated with improved performance (e.g., endurance) (Jeukendrup, 2004). However, the average energy drink contains more than one-quarter of a cup of sugar in one can (or 500 mL) (Higgins, Tuttle, and Higgins, 2010), which far exceeds the daily amount of sugar recommended by the Dietary Guidelines Advisory Committee. Therefore, when consumed in large quantities, energy drinks may be a hidden source of calories. And even if the sugar-free version is consumed, the official position of the Academy of Nutrition and Dietetics is that there is inconclusive evidence to show that replacement of sugar-sweetened beverages with sugar-free versions actually reduces body weight (Academy of Nutrition and Dietetics, 2012).

As noted above, there is a dearth of research concerning the ways in which all the components of energy drinks in conjunction with each other affect performance and health.

Another concern is binge drinking of energy drinks with alcohol, which is a common practice among youth, especially white males in college (Higgins, Tuttle, and Higgins, 2010). This combination can impair cognitive function and, more important, can reduce symptoms of alcohol intoxication. In rare cases, energy drinks have also been linked to death among healthy male adults and psychiatric episodes among individuals with known psychological conditions (Higgins, Tuttle, and Higgins, 2010). The consumption of energy drinks has also been associated with changes in the cardiovascular system as well as a decrease in pain threshold (Higgins, Tuttle, and Higgins, 2010). Given that there is no study documenting the long-term effects of energy drinks, experts recommend that non-athletes restrict their intake to one can per day (i.e., less than 400 mg caffeine per day given that beverages come in various sizes and caffeine loads). Experts also recommend that athletes who exercise for less than an hour should not consume energy drinks for performance-enhancing purposes.

Other Beverages. Other noteworthy beverages are non-alcoholic caffeinated drinks, such as coffee or tea. After water, coffee is the beverage most often consumed around the world (Sadiq-Butt and Sultan, 2011). In the United States, 80 percent of U.S. adults consume caffeine every day, often through coffee consumption (although soda intake is very prevalent) (U.S. Food and Drug Administration, 2007).

There are documented benefits from moderate coffee intake, including lower risk for certain cancers, lower incidence of metabolic syndromes such as diabetes, lower risk of coronary heart disease, and lower risk of Alzheimer's disease and Parkinson's disease; however, the effects regarding Parkinson's disease differ across gender (Sadiq-Butt and Sultan, 2011; Arendash and Cao, 2010). These effects are often attributed to the caffeine in coffee and other high-caffeinated non-alcoholic drinks, such as black teas (Steptoe et al., 2007). Caffeine has been consistently found to positively affect cerebral function, such as cognition in adults and adolescents, and has been found to decrease late-life dementia risk (Biessels, 2010).

Despite the strong evidence from observational studies, more research is needed, given that it is very difficult to isolate caffeine intake from other factors that may be equally important in affecting cognition and other cerebral function (Biessels, 2010; Arendash and Cao, 2010). Research on the effects of caffeine (as found in coffee) suggests that it can be associated with insomnia and coronary complexities (e.g., uneven heart rhythm), and that regular caffeine users can develop a tolerance to caffeine (Sadiq-Butt and Sultan, 2011; Federal Food and Drug Administration, 2007). However, the health benefits of caffeine will not be conferred if intake occurs through caffeinated alcoholic drinks (Sadiq-Butt and Sultan, 2011). Also, certain vulnerable populations, such as children and pregnant women, will likely not benefit from high caffeine consumption (Sadiq-Butt and Sultan, 2011).

Dietary Supplements

The U.S. Food and Drug Administration (2013) defines a dietary supplement as "a product taken by mouth that contains a dietary ingredient intended to supplement the diet" (U.S. Army Public Health Command, undated). The "dietary ingredients" in these products may include vitamins, minerals, herbs or other botanicals, amino acids, and such substances as enzymes, organ tissues, glandulars, and metabolites =However, this report will focus only on "health enhancement dietary supplements," given their high consumption by military populations (e.g., over 65 percent report using this kind of dietary supplement at least once a week) to achieve or maintain high fitness levels. To understand more about military personnel's use of dietary supplements in general, see Greenwood and Oria (2008).

Creatine. Of the health enhancement dietary supplements, creatine is extremely popular, given some evidence that it improves muscle energy and strength. Upon closer examination, use of creatine has been found to be effective only among young men for repetitive bursts of exercise lasting less than 30 seconds (i.e., it has no effect in endurance sports, such as running or swimming) (Tarnopolsky, 2010; Dempsey, Mazzone, and Meurer, 2002; Branch, 2003; Jenkinson and Harbert, 2008). Adverse effects of short-term and long-term creatine use include upset stomach, especially among individuals whose creatine intake is higher than the recommended dosage (Tarnopolsky, 2010).

Ephedra. Another supplement containing stimulants and marketed for muscle building or weight loss is ephedra and ephedrine-like substances (e.g., ma huang) (Greenwood and Oria, 2008; Lieberman et al., 2007). In combination with caffeine, ephedrine appears to produce weight loss (in trials of 1–12 months duration) and has been found to be effective in the management of asthmatic bronchoconstriction and hypotension in various trials (Mayo Clinic, 2012).

However, this particular supplement has also been linked to serious cardiovascular adverse effects (e.g., stroke, myocardial infarction) (Cohen and Ernest, 2010). In fact, the herbal stimulant ma huang was banned in the United States in 2004 after reports of adverse health effects, including death (Cohen and Ernest, 2010).

Other Supplements. Research on civilian populations suggests that some dietary supplements, such as red yeast rice (i.e., an ancient Chinese dietary supplement known as red Koji or Hong Qu), offer lipid-lowering benefits according to several randomized controlled trials (Gordon and Becker, 2011). However, there is an overall dearth of research regarding supplements and specific health outcomes (e.g., few fiber supplements have been studied for physiological effectiveness; therefore, it is best to consume fiber in foods) (Slavin, 2008). Indeed, the evidence report for the Dietary Guidelines Advisory Committee states that a "daily multivitamin/mineral supplement does not offer health benefits to healthy Americans." In addition, the report recommends that Americans be cautious when consuming mineral/vitamin supplements, because they have been associated with harmful effects in some settings.

Dietary Patterns and Behavior

In the final section in this chapter, we focus on what is known about consuming various nutrients in conjunction with each other. Above and beyond single nutrients, the consumption of various nutrients in systematic conjunction can also have an effect on health and well-being (i.e., dietary patterns).

Dietary Approaches to Stop Hypertension. The Dietary Approaches to Stop Hypertension (DASH) diet, based on the DASH studies funded by the National Heart, Lung, and Blood Institute), is a 2,100-calorie eating plan that focuses on reducing saturated fat while also increasing fruits, vegetables, and low-fat or fat-free milk and milk products. Another important focus of DASH is to reduce sodium consumption so that intake should range from 1,500 mg (most effective) to 2,300 mg (Dietary Guidelines Advisory Committee, 2010). DASH has been found to lower blood pressure, improve blood lipids, and reduce CVD risk over the typical American diet (Appel et al., 2003, 2005, 1997; Azadbakht et al., 2005; Dauchet et al., 2007; Forman, Stampfer, and Curhan, 2009; Miller et al., 2002; Nowson, Wattanapenpaiboon, and Pachett, 2009; Nowson et al., 2005; 2004; Sacks et al., 2001; Schulze et al., 2003; Fung et al., 2001, 2008; Heidemann et al., 2008; Hu et al., 2000; Levitan, Wolk, and Mittleman, 2009; Osler et al., 2001; Parikh, Lipsitz, and Natarajan, 2009; Singman et al., 1980).

Mediterranean Diet. Research has also focused on the Mediterranean-style diet, which consists of vegetables, fruits, nuts, olive oil, and grains. It also calls for small amounts of meat and full-fat milk and milk products, and it often includes wine with meals. In most studies, individuals consuming a Mediterranean-style diet have reduced CVD risk factors, reduced incidence of CVD, and a lower rate of total mortality (Knoops et al., 2004; Esposito et al., 2004).

Vegetarian Diet. A vegetarian diet has been consistently associated with lower blood pressure (Hakala and Karvetti, 1989; Rouse et al., 1983; Sciarrone et al., 1993; Margetts et al., 1986), decrease in CVD (Chang-Claude et al., 2005; Fraser, 2005; Key et al., 1998; Mann et al., 1997), and reduced risk of death (Fraser, 2005; Key et al., 1998; Mann et al., 1997). Vegetarians also tend to consume fewer overall calories and have a lower BMI than non-vegetarians (Dietary Guidelines Advisory Committee, 2010).

Diet Density. Dietary energy density (kcal/g [kJ/g]) can have a significant effect on energy intake, independent of either macronutrient composition or palatability, among women under controlled laboratory conditions (Bell et al., 1998), and this effect persists with repeated meals, leading to substantial weight gain if meals are consistently energy-dense. For example, laboratory feeding studies manipulating energy density indicate that individuals consistently consume more energy when presented with foods having a higher energy density than with similar foods having a lower energy density (Rolls, 2009). Further, dietary energy density has been associated with satiety, energy intake, and body weight in healthy individuals (Rolls, 2009). Lowering dietary energy density could provide effective strategies for the prevention and treatment of obesity; however, further research is needed to understand the factors underpinning its effects in real-world settings.

Fast Eating. A recent retrospective longitudinal study found that "fast-eaters," especially 20- to 29-year-olds, were more likely to gain weight. In contrast, a randomized study found no association between eating speed and weight among lean and obese women (Spiegel et al., 1993). Further, a body of work suggests that when individuals can eat at will and eat quickly until satisfactorily full, they will eat more food (and more calories) than if they ate more slowly. Equally important, they have same sense of fullness during the early post-prandial period (Karl, Young, and Montain, 2011). More research is needed to understand how eating speed may be related to rate of weight gain (Tanihara et al., 2011).

Compulsive Eating. Prospective longitudinal studies have found an association between binge eating and an increase in body fat mass in children (Puder and Munsch, 2010) and an increased prevalence of uncontrolled eating behavior in obese children and adolescents (Tanofsky-Kraff et al., 2008). Emotional eating is a key factor in binge-eating disorder (BED) among adults, and adults with BED are more likely to internalize and externalize behavioral problems than individuals without BED (Puder and Munsch, 2010).

Other Dietary Behaviors. Dietary behaviors such as snacking, eating breakfast, and consuming liquid rather than solid foods have been researched, albeit some in more depth than others. We highlight some findings from this research:

- **Eating fast food**: Strong evidence suggests that adults and children who consume fast food are at risk for weight gain, becoming overweight, and obesity, especially those who eat one or more fast food meals a week (Rosenheck, 2008).

- **Portion size**: Strong evidence suggests that serving sizes matter for adults trying to maintain a healthy weight (Gilhooly et al., 2007; Hannum et al., 2004, 2006; Pearcey and De Castro, 2002).

- **Breakfast:** There is inconsistent evidence that skipping breakfast places adults at risk for becoming overweight or obese (Purslow et al., 2008). There is more evidence suggesting that skipping breakfast increases children's risk of becoming overweight or obese, although the evidence is much stronger for adolescents (Crossman, Sullivan, and Benin, 2006; Merten, Williams, and Shriver, 2009; Niemeier et al., 2006).

- **Low-quality snacking (e.g., high in fat):** There is inconsistent evidence that snacking is associated with increased body weight in adults, but many researchers have noted that studies define snacking behaviors in vastly different ways, and this is the driving factor for the inconsistency in findings (U.S. Department of Agriculture and U.S. Department of Health and Human Services, 2010).

- **Frequency of meals**: There is not enough research to suggest that the frequency of eating small meals throughout the day is associated with any particular health outcomes for children, adolescents, and adults (U.S. Department of Agriculture and U.S. Department of Health and Human Services, 2010). The more pressing issue is that meals (whether as a combination of several small ones or three individual meals) should not exceed the daily recommended caloric intake for a given individual.

- **Liquid calories:** Limited research suggests that consuming soup, especially broth or water-based soups, may lead to fewer consumed calories a day and lower body weight over time (Rolls et al., 2005). However, most research focused on liquid nutrition is based on supplementation to ill patients in clinic settings; therefore, there is a dearth of research documenting the effects of popular liquid diets on health outcomes (U.S. Department of Agriculture and U.S. Department of Health and Human Services, 2010).

- **Replacement of added sugars with non-caloric sweeteners**: This dietary behavior reduces caloric intake, but research does not suggest that it helps sustain a healthy body weight over time (U.S. Department of Agriculture and U.S. Department of Health and Human Services, 2010).

- **Food reward philosophy**: Reward-related consumption can lead individuals to exceed the adequate amount of calories, but there is limited research exploring "hedonic" systems in brain influence and food intake. Of the recent studies, some have found that rewarding oneself with unhealthy food may affect the same "brain reward circuitries" that are triggered by drug abuse (Kenny, 2011).

- **Western diet**: A diet characterized by processed or fried foods, refined grains, sugary products, and beer is associated with increased risk for depression and anxiety in women compared to more traditional diets (i.e., those composed of vegetables, fruit, meat, fish, and whole grains) (Jacka et al., 2010). Asian diets in particular (e.g., traditional Japanese dietary patterns that emphasize soybean products, fish, seaweeds, vegetables, fruit, green tea, and meat in limited quantities) may have beneficial effects on cardiovascular health (Shimazu et al., 2007).

Conclusions

This chapter has discussed a wide variety of existing measures of individual food intake and has discussed what is known about the relation of those measures to health outcomes.

When measuring food intake, foods linked to health outcomes should be included (e.g., vegetables, fruits), and intake should be measured with validated and reliable instruments that are appropriate for a given goal (e.g., food frequency questionnaires if the goal is to assess typical dietary patterns). Food intake studies should also assess the role of important micronutrients (e.g., sodium) and supplements, which are often not assessed but which clearly have the potential to affect health outcomes, whether positively or negatively (e.g., a decrease in sodium intake was consistently associated with a decrease in CVD). Further, research suggesting that Omega-3 fatty acids can uniquely affect a myriad of psychological, neurological, and metabolic responses may be important for achieving nutritional fitness.

4. Motivators and Barriers: Psychosocial and Environmental Variables

Nutrition research has documented the difficulties individuals face when attempting to initiate or maintain a healthful diet. Knowing dietary guidelines and their associations with health outcomes has proven to be an insufficient motivator for diet-related behavior changes (Brug, 2008). Indeed, research documents a complex set of psychosocial factors that may inhibit individuals from acting on their intention of adopting healthy eating habits successfully and consistently. The scientific research discusses many constructs that can affect people's ability to eat a healthy diet (e.g., barriers, intentions, knowledge, motivation, religiosity, norms), but the constructs of self-efficacy, social support, and attitudes seem to be particularly important for fruit, vegetable, and fat intake among adults and children (Shaikh et al., 2008).

In this chapter, we focus on two types of factors that can affect individuals' ability to maintain a healthy diet: psychosocial factors, such as self-efficacy and social support, and features of the neighborhood food environment, such as access to full-service supermarkets. For each type of factor, we first discuss available measures and then describe findings from the scientific research concerning the relationship of the factors and health outcomes.

Psychosocial Factors

Measurement of Psychosocial Variables

Increasingly, behavioral intervention research discusses the psychosocial factors that are hypothesized to spark diet-related behavior and change. However, much work is still needed to elucidate the role of psychosocial factors in diet; this need highlights the importance of using valid and reliable measures in this line of research.

One fundamental issue of measurement concerns the definition of key variables. Although studies on nutrition and behavior consistently use similar concepts (e.g., self-efficacy), these concepts are defined in a variety of ways. For example, the concept of self-efficacy derives from Bandura's social cognitive theory and was originally defined as the self-confidence in being able to perform a particular behavior and to overcome the likely barriers in performing that behavior (Bandura, 1997).[5] However, some studies fail to adhere to the original conceptualization (e.g., omitting the barrier component so that measures capture only a person's self-confidence), whereas others do not report the reasons why their conceptualization deviates from the original (Baranowski, Webercullen, and Baranowski, 1999). Different conceptualizations have a direct

---

[5] Also see the companion report on the psychological domain.

25

effect on measurement, since studies will not be using measures that tap into the same constructs systematically.

Another aspect of measurement of psychosocial variables in nutrition research is that many measures consist of truncated versions of larger scales, yet studies fail to analyze the validity or reliability of the shortened version in their samples. Modification of a measure either in length or language can affect the instrument's psychometric properties (Devellis, 2003).

There is also an overreliance on single-item measures, even though comprehensive psychosocial measures have been validated in adult samples, such as the Food Belief Survey (Anderson, Winett, and Wojcik,, 2007; Anderson et al., 2000, 2001). Food Belief Survey measures have been validated across diverse samples and tap a variety of psychosocial contrasts (e.g., social support, self-regulation) through separate subscales, all of which exhibited good to excellent psychometric properties (i.e., alpha .76–.91). Further, the survey evaluates enabling factors (e.g., positive outcome expectancies) as well as potential barriers (e.g., negative outcome expectancies). This feature is particularly desirable, given the tendency to focus on either the positive or negative dimensions.

Multiple measures that tap into a range of psychosocial constructs have been developed and used among children or adolescents. One study tapping a wide range of psychological constructs was the Gimme 5 randomized school trial designed to increase fruit and vegetable intake (Baranowski et al., 2000). Scales measured standard constructs of knowledge (e.g., pretend your family is going out to eat supper at a fast food place. You order a hamburger, fries, and milk shake. How could you add another serving of fruit or vegetables to your meal?), social norms (e.g., most people in my family think that eating three or more servings of vegetables each day is a good thing for me to do), and self-efficacy at eating fruit and vegetables (e.g., I think I can add my favorite fruit to my favorite cereal). The study also used scales that measured snack preferences (e.g., right after school, I prefer to have my favorite fruit or favorite cookie), asking and shopping self-efficacy (e.g., I think I can ask my parent or guardian to buy my favorite fruit the next time she or he goes food shopping), and asking behaviors (e.g., in the last two weeks, did you ask someone in your family to go to a restaurant or fast food place because it serves fruit or vegetables?).

However, even the scales highlighted above have a degree of error, since they are based on self-report. Although self-report is a common way to gain psychosocial data from individuals, some have identified innovative ways in which the self-reported measure could be supplemented by another data collection approach. An example is to measure the concept of preferences via a validated rating scale and through an actual tasting presentation (e.g., having individuals identify their preferences with real choices in front of them). Another would be to assess a person's social support via a rating scale and through social network methodology (Baranowski, Webercullen, and Baranowski, 1999).

Evidence of the Relationship Between Psychosocial Factors and Weight-Related Outcomes

As noted, the majority of research on psychosocial determinants of dietary behavior among adults focuses on fruit and vegetable intake (i.e., behavior) or individuals' intentions to consume fruit and vegetables. The efficacy of prediction varied according to the theoretical framework, with studies using the Social Cognitive Theory and Theory of Planned Behavior frameworks having higher predictive value than multicomponent studies or studies using the Health Behavior Model.

Longitudinal studies found that psychosocial variables had stronger predictive value than cross-sectional studies in relation to fruit and vegetable intake. Interestingly, studies sampling both men and women had higher overall efficacy of prediction of behavior relative to studies sampling only men or only women (Guillaumie, Godin, and Vézina-Im, 2010).

In a recent review of the literature, Guillaumie, Godin, and Vézina-Im (2010) found that the variables most consistently associated with the prediction of fruit and vegetable intake were habit, motivation, and goals beliefs about capabilities and knowledge. These same variables were also meaningful for studies focusing on only fruit intake or vegetable intake; however, for the latter, taste was particularly important in predicting behavior. For studies on intention to eat fruit and vegetables, beliefs about capabilities, beliefs about consequences, and social influences were the most meaningful. These same variables were also consistently associated with the intention to eat fruit and vegetables.

In studies of the psychosocial determinants of dietary outcomes in children and adolescents, fruit, vegetable, and fruit juice intake was also the most common outcome of interest. However, there was more variation than in the literature on adults, with some studies focusing on fat intake, energy intake, sugar snacking, and fiber intake (McClain et al., 2009). We highlight some key findings here:

- **Fruit, vegetable, and juice consumption:** For fruit, vegetable, and juice consumption, perceived "modeling" (i.e., the extent to which the parent engages in a specific dietary behavior as reported by the child) was consistently associated with such consumption, as were liking, knowledge, and preferences. Other variables, including attitude, availability, perceived barriers, outcome expectations, self-efficacy, social desirability, and social support, were not consistently associated with fruit, vegetable, and juice consumption (McClain et al., 2009).
- **Fat intake:** No one psychosocial factor was consistently associated with fat intake, but knowledge and social support were associated with total energy intake.
- **Sugar intake:** Attitudes toward healthy eating and intentions to consume sugar-sweetened snacks and drinks were consistently associated with eating sugar-sweetened snacks (e.g., less consumption of candy with more positive attitudes toward healthy eating), whereas intention to drink soda and perceived modeling was associated with sweetened beverage intake.

- **Fiber intake:** Familial and social support were associated with fiber intake but no other variables. Support was also associated with other healthful dietary behavior (e.g., consumption of low-fat dairy products), in addition to norms, self-efficacy, and perceived modeling. Regarding the latter construct, it should be noted that only perceived modeling, not modeling as reported by a parent, had consistent predictive value with the dietary behaviors in children and adolescents.

Familial stress is another psychological correlate of obesity, specifically childhood obesity (Puder and Munsch, 2010). The hypothesis is that families with chronic sources of stress, such as mental disorders, foment patterns of excessive eating (Puder and Muchsch, 2010). Obese children are also less likely to be able to curb impulsive behavior (i.e., they have less ability to self-regulate), especially children with Attention Deficit Hyperactive Disorder. Further, obese children tend to exhibit depressive symptoms, anxiety, social withdrawal, and isolation (Goodman and Whitaker, 2002; Rofey et al., 2009). The relationship between depression and increased food intake is consistent in samples of children and adolescents (Puder and Munsch, 2010), with many researchers highlighting that it is the chronic stress produced by depression that is related to adverse metabolic responses (Hasler et al., 2005). These correlates of obesity might represent risk factors for future depression (Puder and Munsch, 2010).

Nutrition and the Environment

The growing number of studies attempting to assess specific features of the food environment related to food behaviors and health was sparked by the idea that neighborhood features can affect health. Although this idea has a long history in the social sciences, and various theoretical frameworks have been developed to study associated concepts, emerging public health investigations of the role of the neighborhood environment in eating are very much in their infancy (Die Roux, 2001).

Measurement of Environmental Variables

The emerging public health research predominantly relies on the ecological framework developed by Stokols (Stokols, 1992) and applied by Glanz and colleagues (Glanz et al., 2005). In the original model, the "nutrition environment" comprised four primary areas: (1) *community* food environments (i.e., types and characteristics of available food outlets in a particular geographic area); (2) *organizational* food environments (i.e., features of the home, school, worksites, churches, and health care facilities that can affect diet-related choices); (3) *consumer* food environments (e.g., the characteristics within food outlets, such as the availability, cost, and quality of the food options); and (4) *informational* food environments (i.e., media and advertising available at the meso and macro levels that can influence individual diet-related choices) (Glanz et al., 2005).

Most research on neighborhood effects on diet and diet-related diseases has focused on the organizational, community, and consumer environments. Out of the 48 instruments developed to measure the food environment, 25 measure organizational food environment, 10 measure community environments, 13 measure the informational food environment, and 11 measure the consumer food environment (Ohri-Vachaspati and Leviton, 2010).[6]

The majority of food environment measures, irrespective of domain, have not been tested for reliability, and even fewer have been tested for validity. Reliability and validity data are available for only 25 percent of the total sample of measures, and only 12 percent have been tested for reliability (Ohri-Vachaspati and Leviton, 2010). To address this issue, efforts are under way to develop valid and reliable measures that can be used in multiple populations (e.g., low-income) and by a wide array of people interested in the food environment (e.g., researchers, community organizations). An example of this kind of measure for the *consumer* environment is the Nutrition Environment Measures Surveys (NEMS), a set of instruments to measure the price of healthy and standard food options in various environments (e.g., supermarkets, restaurants). The NEMS is not only comprehensive (i.e., the NEMS Restaurant Measure [NEMS-R] focuses on eight types of food indicators and the NEMS Store Measures [NEMS-S] include 11 measures of retail store nutrition environments) but can easily be tailored to be culturally appropriate for specific community contexts. The measures have been field-tested, have yielded good reliability and validity, and are currently being used in more than 46 research projects (Honeycutt et al., 2010). Compared to the other consumer food environment measures, the NEMS has had more rigorous testing for psychometric properties. It also assesses crucial aspects of the food environment as they relate to diet quality and healthy food choices (e.g., NEMS-S rates the price and availability of 10 indicator food categories and assesses the quality of fresh fruit and vegetables). However, more research is needed to determine the predictive value of this measure in regards to specific dietary behaviors.

A measure of the *community* environment that has been field tested and tailored to the military context has been the Nutrition Environment Tool (NEAT). NEAT was used to develop the Choose Health Options at Work (CHOW) in the U.S. Navy and Marine Corps and Develop Improved Nutrition Environment (DINE) in the U.S. Air Force. Similar to the original NEAT, DINE and CHOW are online tools that measure policies, barriers to access, availability, nutritional quality, and information (Moore, 2005). The original NEAT was developed by the Michigan Health Communities Collaborative to support Michigan citizens in eating healthier (Michigan Healthy Communities Collaborative, undated). Once stakeholders review and complete the assessment, the data can then be used to develop a NEAT Action Plan, a tool that helps individuals prioritize actions to create a healthy environment and also records progress toward individual goals, which can then be evaluated for efficacy. The original NEAT has been tested for reliability and validity and used in multiple settings (Ohri-Vachaspati and Leviton, 2010). Compared to other community food environment measures, the NEAT was among the most desirable measures, given its psychometric properties. It also captures key aspects of the

---

[6] Frequency does not sum to an 48 because some instruments measured multiple food environments

domains of interest (e.g., diet quality, nutritional information). However, it does not measure some key aspects of the food environment, such as price.

For measures in the *organizational* domain, only three were developed for the worksite food environment, and only two have been tested for either reliability or validity. All measure access, availability, and nutrition. However, neither the Organizational Characteristics of Worksite Survey nor the Worksite Environment Measure taps the aspect of quality. Given the importance of diet quality in achieving nutritional fitness, the Checklist of Health Promotion Environments at Worksite would be a better suited measure (Myers, Housemann, and Lovegreen, 2008; Shimotsu et al., 2007; Oldenburg, Harris Sallis, and Owen, 2002).

Last, the two measures in the *informational* domain are focused on media, advertising, and policies in the school environment. However, only the School Food and Beverage Marketing Inventory has been tested for reliability and validity (Samuels and Associates, 2006).

The Association Between the Neighborhood Food Environment and Diet

A major issue concerning research on the built environment is the lack of continuity across studies in their use of metrics and operationalization of the built environment. For studies solely focused on the food environments (n = 22), many use objective metrics derived from such administrative units as census tracts (Grafova et al., 2008; Li et al., 2008; Mehta and Chang, 2008; Morland, Diez Roux, and Wing, 2006; Morland, Wing, and Diez Roux, 2002; Mujahid et al., 2008; Lopez, 2007; Powell et al., 2007; Wang et al., 2007; Inagami et al., 2006; Mobley et al., 2006; Nelson et al., 2006; Simmons et al., 2005; Sturm and Datar, 2005; Burdette and Whitaker, 2004; Maddock, 2004). Some use a Euclidean buffer to measure neighborhoods (i.e., a small area thought to be significantly unique for individuals living in that particular area) (Crawford et al., 2008; Liu et al., 2007; Jeffery et al., 2006), and others simply did not define the concept of neighborhood (Casey et al., 2008; Boehmer et al., 2007; Poortinga, 2006). Most of these metrics derive from data availability rather than any concrete theoretical framework.

There is a growing body of evidence documenting the linkages between the food environments, dietary behaviors, and the body weight of adults and children. One area of research has focused on the effect of supermarkets and other food outlets on diet and increased risk for obesity. Residing closer to a large grocery store or supermarket has been linked to better dietary quality, as well as lower risk of obesity and other risk factors for chronic disease (Morland, Wing, and Diez Roux, 2002; Bodor et al., 2008; Cheadle et al., 1991; Laraia et al., 2004; Moore, Diez Roux, and Brines, 2008; Rose and Richards, 2004; Casagrande et al., 2009; Ford and Dzewaltowski, 2008; Giskes et al., 2007; Holsten, 2009; Jago, Baranowski, and Baranowski, 2007; Kamphuis et al., 2006; Papas et al., 2007; Van Der Horst et al., 2007). Compared with other food stores, supermarkets tend to offer a large variety of high-quality healthful food products at lower cost (Block and Kouba, 2006; Chung and Myers, 1999; Bodor et al., 2008). For example, a study of 2,392 African Americans and 8,231 white Americans aged 49–73 years who were enrolled in the Atherosclerosis Risk in Communities study showed a clear relationship between living in a census tract with at least one supermarket and meeting current federal dietary guidelines for fruit and vegetable intake (Morland et al., 2002). In another study of urban African American women, Zenk and colleagues found that women who shopped at supermarkets consumed fruit and vegetables more often than those who instead shopped at smaller, independent grocers. Further, several studies have shown that better spatial access to a supermarket is related to a reduced risk for obesity (Liu et al., 2007; Morland et al., 2006; Powell et al., 2007). A study of more than 10,000 adults residing in Mississippi, North Carolina, Maryland, and Minnesota found that people living in census tracts with spatial access to supermarkets and grocery stores had the lowest levels of obesity (21 percent) (Morland et al., 2002). The highest levels of obesity (32–40 percent) were observed in census tracts with only small grocery stores or small grocery and convenience stores but no supermarkets, even after controlling for individual-level sociodemographic factors.

The evidence relating to food retail outlets is less consistent for children. That is, some studies show no evidence linking dietary intake to supermarket access but instead show that the distance from home to a convenience store does affect children's dietary patterns (Larson, Story, and Nelson, 2009). Further, recent studies have found that greater access to supermarkets is not associated with healthful dietary behaviors (e.g., consumption of fruits and vegetables) and BMI in children or adolescents (An and Sturm, 2012; Lee, 2012).

Other foci of the food environment literature include the availability of fast food restaurants and food marketing environments. Regarding the former, *there is consistent, albeit a small amount, of research documenting that density of fast food restaurants and convenience stores is related to increased body mass index* (Holsten, 2009; Papas et al., 2007). Research on food marketing suggests that energy-dense, nutrient-poor products are aggressively marketed in the United States, especially in poor urban areas where many low-income individuals reside (Larson, Story, and Nelson, 2009) and among children, which in turn may affect dietary behaviors.

In several countries (e.g., Belgium, Sweden, Norway), the marketing of nutrient-poor food on TV has sparked regulation to restrict the amount of advertising programming viewed by children. However, the United States has chosen to intervene only when advertisements are blatantly deceptive (McGinnis, Gootman, and Kraak, 2006).

Taken together, research on food environments can benefit from the following:

- better measures of food environments
- more theory-driven research
- longitudinal studies, since most findings on the food environment to date are based on cross-sectional and observational data
- use of research on other contexts (i.e., interpersonal) to supplement the findings from food environment studies.

Conclusions

The vast amount of research investigating the relationship between nutrition and health speaks to importance of understanding the multidimensionality of nutrition. The individual and social factors highlighted in this report need to work in tandem to truly achieve a nutritional pattern that foments physical and psychological resilience. The previous chapter discussed evidence linking the intake of certain foods to specific health outcomes.

In this chapter, we built upon that discussion by describing the ways in which dietary intake is *affected simultaneously by psychosocial factors (e.g., self-efficacy) and the food environment.* For example, it is not enough to measure whether a person has the confidence that she/he can consume more fruits and vegetables, but that she/he can do so in the face of barriers (e.g., restricted availability of fresh fruits and produce at a nearby supermarket). It is also important to be mindful that the neighborhood food environment is not the only food environment an individual is exposed to: Measuring the organizational food environment (e.g., work or school food environments) is also crucial, especially in light of the innovative interventions currently under way. It is those interventions that we turn to in the next chapter.

5. Interventions That Promote Nutritional Fitness

In this chapter, we discuss interventions designed to promote nutritional fitness. These include environment-level interventions, context-specific interventions, and individual-level interventions.

Overview

Most diet/nutrition interventions are lifestyle programs designed to modify specific behaviors, such as fruit and vegetable intake. These interventions address a range of target populations, such as school children and employees; however, some programs focus on specific populations, such as faith-based groups (e.g., Body and Soul; Eat for Life; North Carolina Black Churches United for Better Health Project), medically underserved populations (e.g., Little by Little, Parents As Teachers, High 5 Low Fat Program), low-literate individuals (e.g., the Stanford Nutrition Action Program), or overweight/obese individuals (e.g., SHAPEDOWN, DINE Healthy).

The primary outcome of most interventions is a change in weight (e.g., change in BMI) and, to a lesser extent, maintenance of weight loss. Theoretical frameworks, such as the Theory of Planned Behavior and Social Cognitive Theory, dominate most intervention designs, and most assessments of programs are either randomized controlled trials or nonequivalent control/comparison design. The length of most interventions is a year or less; however, large-scale randomized controlled trials can range from 18 months (e.g., Trial of Lifestyle Interventions for Blood Pressure Control) to six years (e.g., Women's Healthy Living and Eating Study, Women's Health Initiative Dietary Modification) (Chapman, 2010). Below, we describe some noteworthy features of interventions at the environmental, community (or context), and individual levels.

Environment-Level Interventions

Increasing access to physical activity and healthful foods is one major way in which an environmental approach can affect individual-level diet and diet-related disease. Despite the enthusiasm over this approach, there is a dearth of research-tested intervention programs. To date, evidence has not demonstrated that increased spatial access to nutritious food is associated with improvements in neighborhood residents' dietary behavior (Cummins et al., 2005). Two studies in the United Kingdom that measured the effect of new or improved large-scale food retail provision in poor communities yielded mixed results, with one study demonstrating a modest improvement in intake among those with the lowest fruit and vegetable intake at baseline (Wrigley, Warm, and Margetts, 2003) and the other finding very little improvement (Cummins et al., 2005). But it is important to note that each of these studies had serious methodological limitations (e.g., the Leeds study did not have a control group and enrolled a non-probability quota sample, and the Glasgow study had a very small sample sizes because of extremely low response rates). Further research is needed to understand the effect of food retail stores in low-income environments, especially in the United States.

Other environmental interventions to improve dietary behaviors include increasing access to farmers' markets and community gardens. These studies have shown modest changes in adults' fruit and vegetable consumption after giving intervention participants coupons to the local farmers' market (Anderson et al., 2001; Anliker, Winne, and Drake, 1992; Herman et al., 2008) *and after providing seniors with a free market basket* (Johnson et al., 2004). Garden-based interventions aimed at youth had an effect on fruit and vegetable intake (Mcaleese and Rankin, 2007; Hermann et al., 2006; Lautenschlager and Smith, 2007), and increased willingness to taste vegetables (Morris and Zidenberg-Cherr, 2002). However, given that interventions with similar design did not find any significant changes in dietary outcomes (Morris, Neustadter, and Zidenberg-Cherr, 2001; Lineberger and Zajicek, 2000; O'Brien and Shoemaker, 2006; Poston, Shoemaker, and Dzewaltowski, 2005; Koch, Waliczek, and Zajicek, 2006), there is insufficient research on the effectiveness of garden-based interventions among youth and adults.

Other environment-level interventions focus on specific aspects of people's daily environments. Based on increasing evidence suggesting that people are constantly encountering (and often internalizing) environmental cues from the environment to overeat (Wansink, 2010), some innovative research is focused on environmental cues. Specifically, researchers are interested in understanding (and changing) those daily cues sparking diet-related behavior, such as the size of plates, structure and variety of food, and physical positioning of food in a given environment (e.g., cookies by the cash register in the cafeteria).

Indeed, there is empirical evidence that eating is an impulsive and frequently automatic behavior that can be stimulated by food cues (Cohen, 2008; Cohen and Farley, 2008; Volkow, 2007; Rogers and Hill, 1989), rather than a conscious, rational thought. Given this impulsive or "mindless" form of eating, researchers are departing from reason-focused approaches (e.g., teach people what is "unhealthy" and they will subsequently "choose" healthier food as a result) to interventions that focus on changing the subtle environmental cues that spark overeating (Wansink, 2010). Strategies include introducing dinnerware and utensils designed to achieve an appropriate portion size rather than teaching people the complexities of calculating portion size (Wansink, 2010). More details about this approach will be discussed in the context-specific section that follows.

Last, health communication campaigns can directly affect individuals in that they infiltrate people's daily environments in a systematic fashion. The effectiveness of the health campaign depends on the health issue (e.g., seatbelt campaigns are far more effective than drug campaigns), with dietary-related messages falling somewhere in the middle of this efficacy continuum (Snyder, 2007). Further research is needed to test the effectiveness of dietary campaigns.

Context-Specific Interventions

Dietary behavior may be affected by giving individuals the tools and resources in settings where they can routinely practice dietary changes. Settings include those where people spend most of their time (e.g., schools, work) or those that afford some unique element to the process of behavior change (e.g., social support in a person's church). Interventions in faith-based communities have focused mostly on African Americans, since cross-sectional data suggest that African American women with strong religious beliefs are more likely to consume fruit and vegetables, report higher interest in consuming fruits and vegetables, and believe that fruits and vegetables confer specific health benefits (Holt et al., 2005; Shatenstein and Ghadirian, 1998). Some noteworthy examples are the Healthy Body/Health Spirit Trial and Body and Soul program, both of which were designed to increase fruit and vegetable consumption and physical activity among African Americans through a culturally appropriate program (e.g., Forgotten Miracles nutritional video, the Healthy Body/Healthy Spirit video and exercise guide, the Eat for Life Cookbook, a gospel workout audio cassette). Although more research is needed in this area, these church-based interventions did have a short-term effect on the daily consumption of fruits and vegetables and weight among participating congregants.

Work is another important setting for behavior change, since most employed Americans spend a substantial part of the daylight hours at work, so that most of their meals are consumed at work. However, the food environment in the workplace is often riddled with unhealthful choices/messages that promote overconsumption. Interventions at worksites sometimes take an environmental approach by modifying some aspect of the food environment, such as reducing portion sizes available in cafeterias, raising prices in vending machines, or providing access to fitness equipment. The results from several environmental interventions show promising results. Specifically, at Dow Chemical, environmental changes at work were significant predictors of successful weight management (Goetzel et al., 2010); Beresford et al. (2010) report long-term increased fruit and vegetable intake among participating employers in Seattle; French et al. (2010) found increased purchases of healthier items from vending machines after changes in offerings and price incentives were made for transit workers.

However, these context-specific approaches are rare, and most workplace interventions focus on individual-level behaviors with low intensity, often emphasizing information/education and with short-term duration (six months or less). Of these interventions, some approach dietary behavior modification through peer education (e.g., 5-a-Day Peer Education Program), tailored computerized programs delivered solely by email (e.g., Program Alive! Worksite Internet Nutrition, nutrition education classes (e.g., The Next Step Worksite for Cancer Screening and Nutrition Intervention), or other group-based counseling (e.g., Promoting Healthy Living: Assessing More Effects).

Other interventions had multiple components. One example is DINE Healthy,[7] a computer software program that provides nutritional education and tools to set and achieve goals at work and home. The DINE Healthy software can be used at home (or even by health professionals) to record present health habits (e.g., food choices) and caloric expenditures based on a range of physical activities. Intervention research consistently shows that using a goal-setting approach, especially if it can be tailored and stylized for a given population, is successful in achieving results. In general, goal-setting in conjunction with a system of accountability seems to be an effective way to spark behavior change.

School-based dietary education interventions make up a substantial portion of the programs designed for children and adolescents. There is insufficient evidence to suggest that school-based nutrition education works, although school-based physical education interventions have consistently affected health outcomes, such as body fat and blood pressure in children and adolescents (e.g., PATH Program, MSPAN). There are also environmentally focused approaches, which are largely driven by the research linking environmental cues to overeating, as described earlier. This approach is very promising in the school context, where environmental cues to overeat are powerful (e.g., availability of energy-dense food in vending machines) (Wansink, 2010). This work has demonstrated that drawing attention to more healthful foods (e.g., making them more accessible, displaying them more prominently) while making unhealthy options less convenient or less visible has been effective in increasing sales of healthful items in school cafeterias (Wansink, 2010).

Although it has yet to be studied in the context of health outcomes, another tactic that has had large success at the lowest cost is requiring that high school students pay cash for desserts and soft drinks, which makes it more difficult than simply buying the item with a debit card or PIN account. Given that many environmental interventions are resource-intense (e.g., opening a new supermarket), it is important that more rigorous research is conducted to understand the effect of interventions using economic-based tactics on such specific health outcomes as obesity.

Finally, there were very few interventions designed to test the effect of family-level resources, such as social support. One example was CARDIAC Kinder, a family-based program for kindergartners designed to promote healthy dietary habits and increase physical activity through positive parental modeling behavior and education. This intervention found that children in the treatment group consumed fewer sweets each week relative to children in the control condition; however, no other dietary behaviors were modified (e.g., fruit and vegetable consumption). More research is needed in this area to understand the role of family and how it may effectively promote healthful dietary behaviors.

---

[7] Note that this is not the same as DINE, which is a tool developed to help Department of Defense communities measure accessibility to healthy food options.

Individual-Level Interventions

Many individual-level interventions employ behavioral counseling to spark changes in dietary patterns. A major characteristic of these interventions is the range of intensity, with some consisting of a single session and others involving more than 20 group sessions over two years. Many of the low-intensity interventions have been implemented in a primary health care setting. These same low-intensity interventions involved disseminating information about healthful diet through the web or mail only, and others supplemented this material with diet-related information disseminated by a health care provider (Lin et al., 2010).

More-intense interventions involved individual counseling (either in person or over the phone) or various group counseling sessions (Lin et al., 2010). Although the intense interventions entailed more resources than the less-intense interventions, only three intense interventions have been designed to detect improvements in cardiovascular disease (Howard et al., 2006; Prentice et al., 2006; Cook et al., 2007). Two out of three found a significant decrease in cardiovascular events among those individuals who received the behavioral counseling.

There were some important differences in findings by type of counseling (i.e., fruits and vegetables only, low-fat, and general heart-healthy). For example, fruits and vegetables only diet counseling was not consistently associated with improvement in any health outcomes but was consistently associated with increased intake of fruits and vegetables (John et al., 2002). Low-fat and general heart-healthy dietary counseling only was consistently associated with reduction in adiposity (Halbert et al., 2000; Anderson et al., 1992; Brekke, Jansson, and Lenner, 2005; Coates et al., 1999; Kristal et al., 2000; Roderick et al., 1997; Sacerdote et al., 2006; Stefanick et al., 1998; Tinker et al., 2008), blood pressure (Hellenius et al., 1993; Stefanick et al., 1998), total cholesterol (Anderson et al., 1992; Stefanick et al., 1998), and glucose tolerance outcomes but only at 12 months (Tinker et al., 2008). Overall, these interventions entailed a large amount of resources with little regard for the context in which individuals needed to make these dietary decisions. It is likely that an individual-level approach could benefit from introducing environment-level components.

Conclusions

This discussion of nutrition interventions focused on programs targeted at three different levels: the environment, the community, and the individual. Environment-level interventions focus on increasing access to healthful foods, modifying consumption cues in one's environment, and introducing health communication campaigns. Context-specific interventions focus on settings where people spend most of their time—work, school, faith-based organizations, etc. Individual-level interventions focus on individual eating behaviors, typically through some type of behavioral counseling of varying intensity. Although some programs and interventions at all three levels have shown promise, more research is needed to assess which programs are most effective in improving nutritional fitness.

6. Conclusions

This report has focused on key domains within the broader construct of nutritional fitness, including individual food intake, food choices and perceived barriers, and the food environment. Perhaps not surprisingly, appropriate intake of essential nutrients is crucial to overall health and well-being, and some specific foodstuffs are consistently associated with positive health outcomes, including fruits, vegetables, whole grains, fat-free and low-fat dairy products, and seafood. Limited caloric intake is also important. It is also crucial to consume fewer foods containing sodium (salt), saturated fats, trans-fats, cholesterol, added sugars, and refined grains (Dietary Guidelines Advisory Committee, 2010). Air Force programs should take heed of these findings and leverage this knowledge to buttress current and future efforts designed to improve resilience through nutrition.

This report also found modest evidence that a healthful diet is shaped by individual-level (e.g., psychosocial) factors and environment-level factors. Although much more work is needed, an important first step is to measure facilitators and barriers at both the individual and environment levels to develop effective interventions that increase nutritional fitness.

Although the Air Force can harness the tools developed to assess nutritional constructs for large populations, it is important to be mindful of the methodological limitations identified in this report. When crafting nutrition-related programs, the Air Force should also carefully consider the evidence in the context of the special nutritional needs of the military population. Such an approach will increase the efficacy of nutrition programs in preventing and mitigating stress and thus ultimately achieve the goal of enhancing resilience.

Bibliography

Abete, I., D. Parra, and J. Martinez, "Energy-Restricted Diets Based on a Distinct Food Selection Affecting the Glycemic Index Induce Different Weight Loss and Oxidative Response," *Journal of Clinical Nutrition,* Vol. 27, No. 4, 2008, pp. 545–551.

Academy of Nutrition and Dietitics, "Use of Nutritive and Nonnutritive Sweeteners," *Journal of the Academy of Nutrition and Dietetics*, Vol. 112, 2012, pp.739–758.

American Heart Association, "Fish and Omega-3 Fatty Acids," September 8, 2010. As of October 18, 2013:
http://www.heart.org/HEARTORG/General/Fish-and-Omega-3-Fatty-Acids_UCM_303248_Article.jsp

An, R., and R. Sturm, "School and Residential Neighborhood Food Environment and Diet Among California Youth," *American Journal of Preventive Medicine*, Vol. 42, No. 2, 2012, pp. 129–135.

Anderson, E. S. , R. A. Winett, and J. R. Wojcik, "Social-Cognitive Determinants of Nutrition Behavior Among Supermarket Food Shoppers: A Structural Equation Analysis," *Health Psychology*, Vol. 19, No. 5, September 2000, pp. 479–486.

Anderson, E., R. Winett, and J. Wojcik, "Self-Regulation, Self-Efficacy, Outcome Expectations, and Social Support: Social Cognitive Theory and Nutrition Behavior," *Annals of Behavioral Medicine,* Vol. 34, No. 3, 2007, pp. 304–312.

Anderson, E., R. Winett, J. Wojcik, S. Winett, and T. Bowden, "A Computerized Social Cognitive Intervention for Nutrition Behavior: Direct and Mediated Effects of Fat, Fiber, Fruits and Vegetables, Self Efficacy and Outcome Expectancies Among Adults," *Annals of Behavioral Medicine,* Vol. 23, 2001, pp. 88–100.

Anderson, J., T. Garrity, C. Wood, S. Whitis, B. Smith, and P. Oeltgen, "Prospective, Randomized, Controlled Comparison of the Effects of Low-Fat and Low-Fat Plus High-Fiber Diets on Serum Lipid Concentrations," *American Journal of Clinical Nutrition,* Vol. 56, 1992, pp. 887–894.

Anliker, J., M. Winne, and L. Drake, "An Evaluation of the Connecticut Farmers' Market Coupon Program," *Journal of Nutrition Education,* Vol. 24, 1992, pp. 185–191.

Appel, L. J., T. J. Moore, E. Obarzanek, W. M. Vollmer, L. Svetkey, F. M. Sacks, G. A. Bray, T. M. Vogt, J. A. Cutler, M. N. Windhauser, P. H. Lin, and N. Karanja, "A Clinical Trial of the Effects of Dietary Patterns on Blood Pressure," *New England Journal of Medicine,* Vol. 336, 1997, pp. 1117–1124.

Appel, L., C. Champagne, D. Harsha, L. Cooper, E. Obarzanek, P. Elmer, V. Stevens, W. Vollmer, P. Lin, L. Svetkey, S. Stedman, and D. Young, "Effects of Comprehensive Lifestyle Modification on Blood Pressure Control: Main Results of the Premier Clinical Trial," *Journal of American Medical Association,* Vol. 289, No. 16, 2003, pp. 2083–2093.

Appel, L. J., F. M. Sacks, V. J. Carey, E. Obarzanek, J. F. Swain, E. R. Miller 3rd, P. R. Conlin, T. P. Erlinger, B. A. Rosner, N. M. Laranjo, J. Charleston, P. McCarron, L. M. Bishop, and OmniHeart Collaborative Research Group, "Effects of Protein, Monounsaturated Fat, and Carbohydrate Intake on Blood Pressure and Serum Lipids: Results of the OmniHeart Randomized Trial," *Journal of the American Medical Association,* Vol. 294, No. 19, November 16, 2005, pp. 2455–2464.

Arendash, G., and C. Cao, "Caffeine and Coffee as Therapeutics Against Alzheimer's Disease," *Journal of Alzheimers Disorder,* Vol. 20, 2010, Suppl 1, pp. S117-S126.

Avenell, A., T. Brown, M. Mcgee, M. Campbell, A. Grant, J. Broom, R. Jung, and W. Smith, "What Are the Long-Term Benefits of Weight Reducing Diets in Adults? A Systematic Review of Randomized Controlled Trials," *Journal of Human Nutrition and Dietetics,* Vol. 17, No. 4, 2004, pp. 317–335.

Azadbakht, L., P. Mirmiran, A. Esmaillzadeh, T. Azizi, and F. Azizi, "Beneficial Effects of a Dietary Approaches to Stop Hypertension Eating Plan on Features of the Metabolic Syndrome," *Diabetes Care,* Vol. 28, No. 12, December 2005, pp. 2823–2831.

Bahrke, M., W. Morgan, and A. Stegner, "Is Ginseng an Ergogenic Aid," *International Journal of Sports, Nutrition, Exercise and Metabolism,* Vol. 19, No. 3, 2009, pp. 298–322.

Bandura, A., *Self-Efficacy: The Exercise of Control*, New York: Worth Publishers, 1997.

Baranowski, T., K. Webercullen, and J. Baranowski, "Psychosocial Correlates of Dietary Intake: Advancing Dietary Intervention," *Annual Reviews of Nutrition,* Vol. 19, 1999, pp. 17–40.

Baranowski, T., M. Davis, K. Resnicow, J. Baranowski, C. Doyle, L. Lin, M. Smith, and D. Want, "Gimme 5 Fruit, Juice, and Vegetables for Fun and Health: Outcome Evaluation," *Health, Education, and Behavior,* Vol. 27, No. 1, 2000, pp. 96–111.

Barclay, A., V. Flood, E. Rochtchina, P. Mitchell, and J. Brand-Miller, "Glycemic Index, Dietary Fiber, and Risk of Type 2 Diabetes in a Cohort of Older Australians," *Diabetes Care,* Vol. 30, No. 11, 2007, pp. 2811–2813.

Bell, E. A., V. H. Castellanos, C. L. Pelkman, M. L. Thorwart, and B. J. Rolls, "Energy Density of Foods Affects Energy Intake in Normal-Weight Women," *American Journal of Clinical Nutrition*, Vol. 67, 1998, pp. 412–420.

Beresford, S,, B, Thompson, S, Bishop, J, Macintyre, D, Mclerran, and Y, Yasui, "Long-Term Fruit and Vegetable Change in Worksites: Seattle 5 a Day Follow-Up," *American Journal of Health Behavior,* Vol. 34, No. 6, November–December, 2010, pp. 707–720.

Bes-Rastrollo, M, M. A. Martínez-González, A. Sánchez-Villegas, C. de la Fuente Arrillaga, and J. A. Martínez, "Association of Fiber Intake and Fruit/Vegetable Consumption with Weight Gain in a Mediterranean Population," *Nutrition,* Vol. 22, No. 5, pp. 504–511, February 24, 2006.

Bes-Rastrollo, M., R. Van Dam, M. Martinez-Gonzalez, T. Li, L. Sampson, and F. Hu, "Prospective Study of Dietary Energy Density and Weight Gain in Women," *American Journal of Clinical Nutrition,* Vol. 88, No. 3, 2008, pp. 769–777.

Biessels, G., "Caffeine, Diabetes, Cognition, and Dementia," *Journal of Alzheimers Disorder,* Vol. 20, 2010 (Suppl 1), pp. S143-S150.

Block, D., and J. Kouba, "A Comparison of the Availability and Affordability of a Market Basket in Two Communities in the Chicago Area," *Public Health Nutrition,* Vol. 9, No. 7, October 2006, pp. 837–845.

Block, G., M. Woods, A. Potosky, and C. Clifford, "Validation of A Self-Administered Diet History Questionnaire Using Multiple Diet Records," *Journal of Clinical Epidemioogy,* Vol. 43, No. 12, 1990, pp. 1327–1335.

Bodor, J., D. Rose, T. Farley, C. Swalm, and S. Scott, "Neighbourhood Fruit and Vegetable Availability and Consumption: The Role of Small Food Stores in an Urban Environment," *Public Health Nutrition,* Vol. 11, 2008, pp. 413–420.

Boehmer, T. K., C. M. Hoehner, A. D. Deshpande, L. K. Brennan Ramirez, and R. C. Brownson, "Perceived and Observed Neighborhood Indicators of Obesity Among Urban Adults," *International Journal of Obesity (London),* 2007.

Branch, J., "Effect of Creatine Supplementation on Body Composition and Performance: A Meta-Analysis," *International Journal of Sports, Nutrition, Exercise and Metabolism,* Vol. 13, No. 2, 2003, pp. 198–226.

Brekke, H., P. Jansson, and R. Lenner, "Long-Term (1- and 2-Year) Effects of Lifestyle Intervention in Type 2 Diabetes Relatives," *Diabetes Research and Clinical Practice,* Vol. 70, 2005, pp. 225–234.

Britz, B., W. Siegfried, A. Ziegler, C. Lamertz, B. Herpertz-Dahlmann, H. Remschmidt, H. Wittchen, and J. Hebebrand, "Rates of Psychiatric Disorders in a Clinical Study Group of Adolescents with Extreme Obesity and in Obese Adolescents Ascertained Via a Population Based Study," *International Journal of Obesity Related and Metabolic Disorders,* Vol. 24, 2000, pp. 1707–1714.

43

Brug, J., "Determinants of Healthy Eating: Motivation, Abilities and Environmental Opportunities," *Family Practice,* Vol. Suppl 1, December 2008, pp. I50–I55.

Buijsse, B., E. Feskens, M. Schulze, N. Forouhi, N. Wareham, S. Sharp, D. Palli, G. Tognon, J. Halkjaer, A. Tjønneland, M. Jakobsen, K. Overvad, R. A. Dl Van De, H. Du, T. Sørensen, and H. Boeing, "Fruit and Vegetable Intakes and Subsequent Changes in Body Weight in European Populations: Results from the Project on Diet, Obesity, and Gene," *American Journal of Clinical Nutrition,* Vol. 90, No. 1, 2009, pp. 202–209.

Burdette, H. L., and R. C. Whitaker, "Neighborhood Playgrounds, Fast Food Restaurants, and Crime: Relationships to Overweight in Low-Income Preschool Children," *Preventative Medicine,* Vol. 38, No. 1, 2004, pp. 57–63.

Butki, B., J. Baumstark, and S. Driver, "Effects of a Carbohydrate-Restricted Diet on Affective Responses to Acute Exercise Among Physically Active Participants," *Perceptual and Motor Skills Journal,* Vol. 96, 2003, pp. 607–615.

Cade, J., R. Thompson, V. Burley, and D. Warm, "Development, Validation and Utilisation of Food-Frequency Questionnaires—A Review," *Public Health Nutrition,* Vol. 5, No. 4, 2002, pp. 567–587.

Carithers, T., S. Talegawkar, M. Rowser, O. Henry, P. Dubbert, M. Bogle, H. Taylor, Jr., and K. Tucker, "Validity and Calibration of Food Frequency Questionnaires Used with African-American Adults in the Jackson Heart Study," *Journal of American Diet Association,* Vol. 109, No. 7, 2009, pp. 1184–1193.

Casagrande, S. S., M. C. Whitt-Glover, K. J. Lancaster, A. M. Odoms-Young, and T. L. Gary, "Built Environment and Health Behaviors Among African Americans: A Systematic Review," *American Journal of Preventive Medicine,* Vol. 36, No. 2, 2009, pp. 174–181.

Casey, A. A., M. Elliott, K. Glanz, D. Haire-Joshu, S. L. Lovegreen, B. E. Saelens, J. F. Sallis, and R. C. Brownson, "Impact of the Food Environment and Physical Activity Environment on Behaviors and Weight Status in Rural US Communities," *Preventative Medicine,* Vol. 47, No. 6, 2008, pp. 600–604.

Centers for Disease Control and Prevention, *Vitamins and Minerals*, Atlanta, Ga., February 23, 2011.

Chang-Claude, J., S. Hermann, U. Eilber, and K. Steindorf, "Lifestyle Determinants and Mortality in German Vegetarians and Health-Conscious Persons: Results of a 21-Year Follow-Up," *Cancer Epidemiology Biomarkers Preview,* Vol. 14, No. 4, April 2005, pp. 963–968.

Chapman, K., "Can People Make Healthy Changes to Their Diet and Maintain Them in the Long Term?" *Appetite,* Vol. 54, No. 3, June 2010, pp. 433–441.

Cheadle, A., B. Psaty, S. Curry, E. Wagner, P. Diehr, T. Koepsell, and A. Kristal, "Community-Level Comparisons Between the Grocery Store Environment and Individual Dietary Practices," *Preventative Medicine,* Vol. 20, No. 2, March 1991, pp. 250–261.

Chen, H., E. O'Reilly, M. L. McCullough, C. Rodriguez, M. A. Schwarzschild, E. E. Calle, M. J. Thun, and A. Ascherio, "Consumption of Dairy Products and Risk of Parkinson's Disease," *American Journal of Epidemiology*, Vol. 165, No. 9, 2007, pp. 998–1006.

Chung, C., and S. L. Myers, Jr., :Do the Poor Pay More for Food? An Analysis of Grocery Store Availability and Food Price Disparities," *The Journal of Customer Affairs,* Vol. 33, No. 2, 1999, pp. 276–296.

Coates, R., D. Bowen, A. Kristal, Z. Feng, A. Oberman, W. Hall, V. George, C. Lewis, M. Kestin, M. Davis, M. Evans, J. Grizzle, and C. Clifford, "The Women's Health Trial Feasibility Study in Minority Populations: Changes in Dietary Intakes," *American Journal of Epidemiology,* Vol. 149, 1999, pp. 1104–1112.

Cobiac, L. J., T. Vos, and J. Lennert Veerman, "Cost-Effectiveness of Interventions to Promote Fruit and Vegetable Consumption," *Plos One,* Vol. 5, No. 11, 2010.

Cohen, D. A., "Neurophysiological Pathways to Obesity: Below Awareness and Beyond Individual Control," *Diabetes,* Vol. 57, 2008, pp. 1768–1773.

Cohen, D. A., and T. Farley, "Eating As An Automatic Behavior," *Preventing Chronic Disease,* Vol. 5, No. 1, 2008.

Cohen, P. A., and E. Ernst, "Safety of Herbal Supplements: A Guide for Cardiologists," *Cardiovasc Therapeutics,* Vol. 28, No. 4, August 2010, pp. 246–253.

Cook, N. R., J. A. Cutler, E. Obarzanek, J. E. Buring, K. Rexrode, S. K. Kumanyika, L. J. Appel, and P. K. Whelton, "Long Term Effects of Dietary Sodium Reduction on Cardiovascular Disease Outcomes: Observational Follow-Up of the Trials of Hypertension Prevention," *British Medical Journal,* Vol. 334, 2007, pp. 885–888.

Craig, W. J., "Health Effects of Vegan Diets," *American Journal of Clinical Nutrition,* Vol. 89, No. 5, May 2009, pp. 1627s–1633s.

Crawford, D. A., A. F. Timperio, J. A. Salmon, L. Baur, B. Giles-Corti, R. J. Roberts, M. L. Jackson, N. Andrianopoulos, and K. Ball, "Neighbourhood Fast Food Outlets and Obesity in Children and Adults: The Clan Study," *International Journal of Pediatric Obesity,* Vol. 3, No. 4, 2008, pp. 249–256.

Crossman, A., D. Sullivan, and M. Benin, "The Family Environment and American Adolescents' Risk of Obesity As Young Adults," *Social Science & Medicine,* Vol. 63, No. 9, 2006, pp. 2255–2267.

45

Cummins, S., M. Petticrew, L. Sparks, and A. Findlay, "Large Scale Food Retail Interventions and Diet," *British Medical Journal,* Vol. 330, No. 7493, March 26, 2005, pp. 683–684.

Dale, K., K. McAuley, R. Taylor, S. Williams, V. Farmer, P. Hansen, S. Vorgers, A. Chisholm, and J. Mann, "Determining Optimal Approaches for Weight Maintenance: A Randomized Controlled Trial," *Canadian Medical Association Journal,* Vol. 180, No. 10, 2009, pp. E39–46.

Dauchet, L., E. Kesse-Guyot, S. Czernichow, S. Bertrais, C. Estaquio, S. Péneau, A. Vergnaud, S. Chat-Yung, K. Castetbon, V. Deschamps, P. Brindel, and S. Hercberg, "Dietary Patterns and Blood Pressure Change over 5-Y Follow-Up in the Su.Vi.Max Cohort," *American Journal of Clinical Nutrition,* Vol. 85, No. 6, June 2007, pp. 1650–1656.

Davis, J., V. Hodges, and M. Gillham, "Normal-Weight Adults Consume More Fiber and Fruit Than Their Age- and Height-Matched Overweight/Obese Counterparts," *Journal of American Diet Association,* Vol. 106, No. 6, 2006, pp. 833–840.

DCoE—*See* Defense Centers of Excellence.

Defense Centers of Excellence for Psychological Health and Traumatic Brain Injury (DCoE), Tramatic Brain Injury, 2011. As of April 9, 2011: http://wsw.dcoe.health.mil/

De Rougemont, A., S. Normand, J. Nazare, M. Skilton, M. Sothier, S. Vinoy, and M. Laville, "Beneficial Effects of a 5-Week Low-Glycemic Index Regimen on Weight Control and Cardiovascular Risk Factors in Overweight Non-Diabetic Subjects," *British Journal of Nutrition,* Vol. 98, No. 6, 2007, pp. 1288–1298.

Deierlein, A., A. Siega-Riz, and A. Herring, "Dietary Energy Density But Not Glycemic Load Is Associated with Gestational Weight Gain," *American Journal of Clinical Nutrition,* Vol. 88, No. 3, 2008, pp. 693–699.

Dempsey, R., M. Mazzone, and L. Meurer, "Does Oral Creatine Supplementation Improve Strength? A Meta-Analysis," *Journal of Family Practice,* Vol. 51, No. 11, November 2002, pp. 945–951.

Devellis, R. F., *Scale Development: Theory and Application*, 2nd Ed., Thousand Oaks, Calif.: Sage Publications, 2003.

DiCastelnuevoC., A. S. Costanzo, V. Bagnardi, M. Donati, L. Iiacoviello, and G. De Gaetano, "Alcohol Dosing and Total Mortality in Men and Women: An Updated Meta-Analysis of 34 Prospective Studies," *Archives of Internal Medicine,* Vol. 166, No. 22, December 11–25, 2006, pp. 2437–2445.

Dietary Guidelines Advisory Committee, *Evidence Report for the Dietary Guidelines for Americans 2010*, 2010. As of September 23, 2011: http://Www.Cnpp.Usda.Gov/Dgas2010-Dgacreport.Htm

Diez Roux, A. V., "Investigating Neighborhood and Area Effects on Health," *American Journal of Public Health,* Vol. 91, No. 11, November 2001, pp. 1783–1789.

Donaldson, C., T. Perry, and M. Rose, "Glycemic Index and Endurance Performance," *International Journal of Sports, Nutrition, Exercise and Metabolism,* Vol. 20, No. 2, 2010, pp. 154–165.

Due, A., T. Larsen, H. Mu, K. Hermansen, S. Stender, and A. Astrup, "Comparison of 3 Ad Libitum Diets for Weight-Loss Maintenance, Risk of Cardiovascular Disease, and Diabetes: A 6-Mo Randomized, Controlled Trial," *American Journal of Clinical Nutrition,* Vol. 88, No. 5, November 2008, pp. 1232–1241.

Elkind, M., R. Sciacca, B. Boden-Albala, T. Rundek, M. Paik, and R. Sacco, "Moderate Alcohol Consumption Reduces Risk of Ischemic Stroke: The Northern Manhattan Study," *Stroke,* Vol. 37, No. 1, November 23, 2005, pp. 13–19.

Emberson, J., A. Shaper, S. Wannamethee, R. Morris, and P. Whincup, "Alcohol Intake in Middle Age and Risk of Cardiovascular Disease and Mortality: Accounting for Intake Variation over Time," *American Journal of Epidemiology,* Vol. 161, No. 9, May 1, 2005, pp. 856–863.

Esposito, K., R. Marfella, M. Ciotola, C. Di Palo, F. Giugliano, G. Giugliano, M. D'armiento, F. D'andrea, and D. Giugliano, "Effect of a Mediterranean-Style Diet on Endothelial Dysfunction and Markers of Vascular Inflammation in the Metabolic Syndrome: A Randomized Trial," *Journal of American Medical Association,* Vol. 292, No. 12, September 22, 2004, pp. 1440–1446.

Federal Food and Drug Administration, "Medicines in My Home: Caffeine and Your Body," 2007. As of September 22, 2011: http://www.Fda.Gov/Downloads/Drugs/Resourcesforyou/Consumers/Buyingusingmedicinesafely/Understandingover-The-Countermedicines/Ucm205286.Pdf

Flórez, K. R., R. A. Shih, and M. T. Martin, *Nutritional Fitness and Resilience: A Review of Relevant Constructs, Measures, and Links to Well-Being.* Santa Monica, Calif.: RAND Corporation, RR-105-AF, 2014. As of October 2014: http://www.rand.org/pubs/research_reports/RR105.html

Ford, P., and D. Dzewaltowski, "Disparities in Obesity Prevalence Due to Variation in the Retail Food Environment: Three Testable Hypotheses," *Nutrition Review,* Vol. 66, No. 4, April 2008, pp. 216–218.

Forman, J., M. Stampfer, and G. Curhan, "Diet and Lifestyle Risk Factors Associated with Incident Hypertension in Women," *Journal of American Medical Association,* Vol. 302, No. 4, July 2009, pp. 401–411.

Fraser, G. E., "A Comparison of First Event Coronary Heart Disease Rates in Two Contrasting California Populations," *Journal of Nutritional Health and Aging* Vol. 9, No. 1, 2005, pp. 53–58.

French, S., L. Harnack, P. Hannan, N. Mitchell, A. Gerlach, and T. Toomey, "Worksite Environment Intervention to Prevent Obesity Among Metropolitan Transit Workers," *Preventative Medicine,* Vol. 50, No. 4, April 2010, pp. 180–185.

Frisch, S., A. Zittermann, H. Berthold, C. Götting, J. Kuhn, K. Kleesiek, P. Stehle, and H. Körtke, "A Randomized Controlled Trial on the Efficacy of Carbohydrate-Reduced Or Fat-Reduced Diets in Patients Attending a Telemedically Guided Weight Loss Program," *Cardiovascular Diabetology,* Vol. 8, No. 36, July 18, 2009.

Fujioka, K., F. Greenway, J. Sheard, and Y. Ying, "The Effects of Grapefruit on Weight and Insulin Resistance: Relationship to the Metabolic Syndrome," *Journal of Medical Food,* Vol. 9, No. 1, 2006, pp. 49–54.

Fung, T. T. , W. C. Willett, M. J. Stampfer, J. E. Manson, and F. B. Hu, "Dietary Patterns and the Risk of Coronary Heart Disease in Women," *Archives of Internal Medicine*, Vol. 161, No. 15, August 13–27, 2001, pp. 1857–1862.

Fung, T., S. Chiuve, M. Mccullough, K. Rexrode, G. Logroscino, and F. Hu, "Adherence to a Dash-Style Diet and Risk of Coronary Heart Disease and Stroke in Women," *Archives of Internal Medicine,* Vol. 168, No. 7, April 14, 2008, pp. 713–720.

Gardner, C., A. Kiazand, S. Alhassan, S. Kim, R. Stafford, R. Balise, H. Kraemer, and A. King, "Comparison of the Atkins, Zone, Ornish, and Learn Diets for Change in Weight and Related Risk Factors Among Overweight Premenopausal Women: The a to Z Weight Loss Study: A Randomized Trial," *Journal of American Medical Association,* Vol. 297, No. 2, March 7, 2007, pp. 969–977.

Gardner, T. W., T. J. Dishion, and A. M. Connell, "Adolescent Self-Regulation as Resilience: Resistance to Antisocial Behavior Within the Deviant Peer Context," *Journal of Abnormal Child Psychology,* Vol. 36, No. 2, February 2008, pp. 273–284.

Genkinger, J., E. Platz, S. Hoffman, G. Comstock, and K. Helzlsouer, "Fruit, Vegetable, and Antioxidant Intake and All-Cause, Cancer, and Cardiovascular Disease Mortality in a Community-Dwelling Population in Washington County," *American Journal of Epidemiology,* Vol. 160, No. 12, December 15, 2004, pp. 1223–1233.

Gilhooly, C., S. Das, J. Golden, M. Mccrory, G. Dallal, E. Saltzman, F. Kramer, and S. Roberts, "Food Cravings and Energy Regulation: The Characteristics of Craved Foods and Their Relationship with Eating Behaviors and Weight Change During 6 Months of Dietary Energy Restriction," *International Journal of Obesity,* Vol. 31, No. 12, 2007, pp. 1849–1858.

Giskes, K., F. Van Lenthe, J. Brug, J. Mackenbach, and G. Turrell, "Socioeconomic Inequalities in Food Purchasing: The Contribution of Respondent-Perceived and Actual (Objectively Measured) Price and Availability of Foods," *Preventative Medicine,* Vol. 45, No. 1, July 2007, pp. 41–48.

Glanz, K., J. F. Sallis, B. E. Saelens, and L. D. Frank, "Healthy Nutrition Environments: Concepts and Measures," *American Journal of Health Promotion,* Vol. 19, No. 5, 2005, pp. 330–333.

Goetzel, R., E. Roemer, X. Pei, M. Short, M. Tabrizi, M. Wilson, D. Dejoy, B. Craun, K. Tully, J. White, and C. Baase, "Second-Year Results of An Obesity Prevention Program at the Dow Chemical Company," *Journal of Occupation, Environment, and Medicine,* Vol. 52, No. 3, March 2010, pp. 291–302.

Gómez-Pinilla, F., "Brain Foods: The Effects of Nutrients on Brain Function," *National Review of Neuroscience,* Vol. 9, No. 7, July 2008, pp. 568–578.

———, "The Combined Effects of Exercise and Foods in Preventing Neurological and Cognitive Disorders," *Preventative Medicine,* Vol. 52, No. 1 (Suppl.), pp. S75–S80, June 2011.

Goodman, E., and R. Whitaker, "A Prospective Study of the Role of Depression in the Development and Persistence of Adolescent Obesity," *Pediatrics,* Vol. 110, 2002, pp. 497–504.

Gordon, R., and D. Becker, "The Role of Red Yeast Rice for the Physician," *Current Atherosclerosis Reports,* Vol. 13, No. 1, February 2011, pp. 73–80.

Goss, J., and L. Grubbs, "Comparative Analysis of Body Mass Index, Consumption of Fruits and Vegetables, Smoking, and Physical Activity Among Florida Residents," *Journal of Community Health Nursing,* Vol. 22, No. 1, 2005, pp. 37–46.

Grafova, I. B., V. A. Freedman, R. Kumar, and J. Rogowski, "Neighborhoods and Obesity in Later Life," *American Journal of Public Health,* Vol. 98, No. 11, 2008, pp. 2065–2071.

Greenwood, M.R.C., and Maria Oria, eds., "Use of Dietary Supplements by Military Personnel," National Academy of Sciences, The National Academies Press, 2008. As of November 13, 2013:
http://www.nap.edu/catalog.php?record_id=12095

Guillaumie, L., G. Godin, and L. Vézina-Im, "Psychosocial Determinants of Fruit and Vegetable Intake in Adult Population: A Systematic Review," *International Journal of Behavior, Nutrition, and Physical Activity,* Vol. 7, No. 12, February 2, 2010.

Hakala, P., and R. Karvetti, "Weight Reduction on Lactovegetarian and Mixed Diets. Changes in Weight, Nutrient Intake, Skinfold Thicknesses and Blood Pressure," *European Journal of Clinical Nutrition,* Vol. 43, No. 6, June 1989, pp. 421–430.

Halbert, J., C. Silagy, P. Finucane, R. Withers, and P. Hamdorf, "Physical Activity and Cardiovascular Risk Factors: Effect of Advice from an Exercise Specialist in Australian General Practice," *Medical Journal of Australia,* Vol. 173, 2000, pp. 84–87.

Halton, T., W. Willett, S. Liu, J. Manson, M. Stampfer, and F. Hu, "Potato and French Fry Consumption and Risk of Type 2 Diabetes in Women," *American Journal of Clinical Nutrition,* Vol. 83, No. 2, February 2006a, pp. 284–290.

Halton, T. L., W. C. Willett, S. Liu, J. E. Manson, C. M. Albert, K. Rexrode, and F. B. Hu, "Low-Carbohydrate-Diet Score and the Risk of Coronary Heart Disease in Women," *New England Journal of Medicine*, Vol. 355, No. 19, November 9, 2006b, pp. 1991–2002. PubMed PMID: 17093250.

Hannum, S., L. Carson, E. Evans, K. Canene, E. Petr, L. Bui, and J. Erdman, "Use of Portion-Controlled Entrees Enhances Weight Loss in Women," *Obesity Research,* Vol. 12, No. 3, 2004, pp. 538–546.

Hannum, S. M., L. A. Carson, E. M. Evans, E. L. Petr, C. M. Wharton, L. Bui, and J. W. Erdman, Jr., "Use of Packaged Entrees as Part of a Weight-Loss Diet in Overweight Men: An 8-Week Randomized Clinical Trial," *Diabetes, Obesity, and Metabolism*, Vol. 8, No. 2, March 2006, pp. 146–155

Hare-Bruun, H., A. Flint, and B. Heitmann, "Glycemic Index and Glycemic Load in Relation to Changes in Body Weight, Body Fat Distribution, and Body Composition in Adult Danes," *American Journal of Clinical Nutrition,* Vol. 84, No. 4, 2006, pp. 871–879.

Hasler, G., D. Pine, D. Kleinbaum, A. Gamma, D. Luckenbaugh, V. Ajdacic, D. Eich, W. Rossler, and J. Angst, "Depressive Symptoms During Childhood and Adult Obesity: The Zurich Cohort Study," *Molecular Psychiatry,* Vol. 10, 2005, pp. 842–850.

He, K., F. Hu, G. Colditz, J. Manson, W. Willett, and S. Liu, "Changes in Intake of Fruits and Vegetables in Relation to Risk of Obesity and Weight Gain Among Middle-Aged Women," *International Journal of Obesity Related and Metabolic Disorders,* Vol. 28, No. 12, 2004, pp. 1569–1574.

Heidemann, C., M. Schulze, O. Franco, R. Van Dam, C. Mantzoros, and F. Hu, "Dietary Patterns and Risk of Mortality from Cardiovascular Disease, Cancer, and All Causes in a Prospective Cohort of Women," *Circulation,* Vol. 118, No. 3, July 15, 2008, pp. 230–237.

Hellenius, M., U. De Faire, B. Berglund, A. Hamsten, and I. Krakau, "Diet and Exercise Are Equally Effective in Reducing Risk for CVD: Results of a Randomized Controlled Study in Men With Slightly to Moderately Raised Cardiovascular Risk Factors," *Atherosclerosis,* Vol. 103, 1993, pp. 81–91.

Herman, D., G. Harrison, A. Afifi, and E. Jenks, "Effect of a Targeted Subsidy on Intake of Fruits and Vegetables Among Low-Income Women in the Special Supplemental Nutrition Program for Women, Infants, and Children," *American Journal of Public Health,* Vol. 98, 2008, pp. 98–105.

Hermann, J., S. Parker, B. Brown, Y. Siewe, B. Denney, and S. Walker, "After-School Gardening Improves Children's Reported Vegetable Intake and Physical Activity," *Journal of Nutrition, Education, and Behavior,* Vol. 38, 2006, pp. 201–202.

Higgins, J., T. Tuttle, and C. Higgins, "Energy Beverages: Content and Safety," *Mayo Clinic Proceedings,* Vol. 85, No. 11, November 2010, pp. 1033–1041.

Hodge, A., D. English, K. O'Dea, and G. Giles, "Glycemic Index and Dietary Fiber and the Risk of Type 2 Diabetes," *Diabetes Care,* Vol. 27, No. 11, 2004, pp. 2701–2706.

Holsten, J., "Obesity and the Community Food Environment: A Systematic Review," *Public Health Nutrition,* Vol. 12, No. 3, 2009, pp. 397–405.

Holt, C., D. Haire-Joshu, S. Lukwago, L. Lewellyn, and M. Kreuter, "The Role of Religiosity in Dietary Beliefs and Behaviors Among Urban African American Women," *Cancer Control,* Vol. 12, No. 2, Suppl., 2005, pp. 84–90.

Honeycutt, S., E. Davis, M. Clawson, and K. Glanz, "Training for and Dissemination of the Nutrition Environment Measures Surveys (NEMS)," *Preventing Chronic Disease,* Vol. 7, No. 6, November 2010, P. A126.

Howard, B., L. Van Horn, J. Hsia, et al., "Low-Fat Dietary Pattern and Risk of CVD: The Women's Health Initiative Randomized Controlled Dietary Modification Trial," *Journal of American Medical Association,* Vol. 295, 2006, pp. 655–666.

Hu, F., E. Rimm, M. Stampfer, A. Ascherio, D. Spiegelman, and W. Willett, "Prospective Study of Major Dietary Patterns and Risk of Coronary Heart Disease in Men," *American Journal of Clinical Nutrition,* Vol. 72, No. 4, October 2000, pp. 912–921.

Hui, L., and E. Nelson, "Meal Glycemic Load of Normal-Weight and Overweight Hong Kong Children," *European Journal of Clinical Nutrition,* Vol. 60, No. 2, 2006, pp. 220–227.

Hung, H., K. Joshipura, R. Jiang, F. Hu, D. Hunter, S. Smith-Warner, G. Colditz, B. Rosner, D. Spiegelman, and W. Willett, "Fruit and Vegetable Intake and Risk of Major Chronic Disease," *Journal of National Cancer Institute,* Vol. 96, No. 21, November 2004, pp. 1557–1584.

Inagami, S., D. A. Cohen, B. K. Finch, and S. M. Asch, "You Are Where You Shop Grocery Store Locations, Weight, and Neighborhoods," *American Journal of Preventive Medicine,* Vol. 31, 2006, pp. 10-17.

Jacka, F. N., J. A. Pasco, A. Mykletun, L. J. Williams, A. M. Hodge, S. L. O'Reilly, G. C. Nicholson, M. A. Kotowicz, and M. Berk, "Association of Western and Traditional Diets With Depression and Anxiety in Women," *American Journal of Psychiatry,* Vol. 167, No. 3, 2010, pp. 305–311.

Jago, R., T. Baranowski, and J. Baranowski, "Fruit and Vegetable Availability: A Micro Environmental Mediating Variable?" *Public Health Nutrition,* Vol. 10, No. 7, 2007, pp. 681–689.

Jeffery, R. W., J. Baxter, M. Mcguire, and J Linde, "Are Fast Food Restaurants An Environmental Risk Factor for Obesity?"" *The International Journal of Behavioral Nutrition and Physical Activity,* Vol. 3, No. 2, 2006.

Jenab, M., N. Slimani, M. Bictash, P. Ferrari, and S. Bingham, "Biomarkers in Nutritional Epidemiology: Applications, Needs and New Horizons," *Human Genetics,* Vol. 125, No. 5-6, April 9, 2009, pp. 507–525.

Jenkinson, D., and A. Harbert, "Supplements and Sports," *American Family Physician,* Vol. 78, No. 9, November 1, 2008, pp. 1039–1046.

Jeukendrup, A. E, "Carbohydrate Intake During Exercise and Performance," *Nutrition*, Vol. 20, 2004, pp. 669–677.

John, J., S. Ziebland, P. Yudkin, L. Roe, and H. Neil, "Oxford Fruit and Vegetable Study Group. Effects of Fruit and Vegetable Consumption on Plasma Antioxidant Concentrations and Blood Pressure: A Randomized Controlled Trial," *Lancet,* Vol. 359, 2002, pp. 1969–1974.

Johnson, D., S. Beaudoin, L. Smith, S. Beresford, and J. Logerfo, "Increasing Fruit and Vegetable Intake in Homebound Elders: The Seattle Senior Farmers' Market Nutrition Pilot Program," *Preventing Chronic Disease,* Vol. 1, No. A03, 2004.

Joshipura, K., H. Hung, T. Li, F. Hu, E. Rimm, M. Stampfer, G. Colditz, and W. Willett, "Intakes of Fruits, Vegetables and Carbohydrate and the Risk of CVD," *Public Health Journal,* Vol. 12, No. 1, January 2009, pp. 115–121.

Just, D. R., and B. Wansink, "Smarter Lunchrooms: Using Behavioral Economics to Improve Meal Selection," *Choices,* Vol. 24, No. 3, 2009.

Kamphuis, C., K. Giskes, G. De Bruijn, W. Wendel-Vos, J. Brug, and F. Van Lenthe, "Environmental Determinants of Fruit and Vegetable Consumption Among Adults: A Systematic Review," *British Journal of Nutrition,* Vol. 96, No. 4, 2006, pp. 620–635.

Karl, P. J., A. J. Young, and S. J. Montain, "Eating Rate During Fixed-Portion Meal Does Not Affect Postprandial Appetite and Gut Peptides or Energy Intake During a Subsequent Meal," *US Army Research*, Paper 131, 2011.

Karlic, H., and A. Lohninger, "Supplementation of L-Carnitine in Athletes: Does It Make Sense?" *Nutrition,* Vol. 20, 2004, pp. 709–715.

Kelley, G. A., K. S. Kelley, and B. Franklin, "Aerobic Exercise and Lipids and Lipoproteins in Patients with Cardiovascular Disease: A Meta-Analysis of Randomized Controlled Trials," *Journal of Cardiopulmonary Rehabilitation*, Vol. 26, No. 3, May–June 2006, pp. 131–139; quiz pp. 140–141, discussion pp. 142–144.

Kelly, S., C. Summerbell, A. Brynes, V. Whittaker, and G. Frost, "Wholegrain Cereals for Coronary Heart Disease," *Cochrane Database System Review,* Vol. 2, 2007.

Kenny, P., "Reward Mechanisms in Obesity: New Insights and Future Directions," *Neuron,* Vol. 69, No. 4, February 24, 2011, pp. 664–679.

Key, T., G. Fraser, M. Thorogood, P. Appleby, V. Beral, G. Reeves, M. Burr, J. Chang-Claude, R. Frentzel-Beyme, J. Kuzma, J. Mann, and K. Mcpherson, "Mortality in Vegetarians and Non-Vegetarians: A Collaborative Analysis of 8300 Deaths Among 76,000 Men and Women in Five Prospective Studies," *Public Health Nutrition,* Vol. 1, No. 1, March 1998, pp. 33–41.

Kiecolt-Glaser, J. K., "Stress, Food, and Inflammation: Psychoneuroimmunology and Nutrition at the Cutting Edge," *Psychosomatic Medicine,* Vol. 72, No. 4, May 2010, pp. 365–369.

Knoops, K., L. De Groot, D. Kromhout, A. Perrin, O. Moreiras-Varela, A. Menotti, and W. Van Staveren, "Mediterranean Diet, Lifestyle Factors, and 10-Year Mortality in Elderly European Men and Women: The Hale Project," *Journal of American Medical Association,* Vol. 292, No. 12, September 22, 2004, pp. 1433–1439.

Koch, S., T. Waliczek, and J. Zajicek, "The Effect of a Summer Garden Program on the Nutritional Knowledge, Attitudes, and Behaviors of Children," *Hort Technology,* Vol. 16, 2006, pp. 620–624.

Koh-Banerjee, P., N. Chu, D. Spiegelman, B. Rosner, G. Colditz, W. Willett, and E. Rimm, "Prospective Study of the Association of Changes in Dietary Intake, Physical Activity, Alcohol Consumption, and Smoking with 9-Y Gain in Waist Circumference Among 16,587 U.S. Men," *American Journal of Clinical Nutrition,* Vol. 78, No. 4, October 2003, pp. 719–727.

Krishnan, S., L. Rosenberg, M. Singer, F. Hu, L. Djoussé, L. Cupples, and J. Palmer, "Glycemic Index, Glycemic Load, and Cereal Fiber Intake and Risk of Type 2 Diabetes in U.S. Black Women," *Archives of Internal Medicine,* Vol. 167, No. 21, 2007, pp. 2304–2309.

Kristal, A., S. Curry, A. Shattuck, Z. Feng, and S. Li, "A Randomized Trial of a Tailored, Self-Help Dietary Intervention: The Puget Sound Eating Patterns Study," *Preventative Medicine,* Vol. 31, 2000, pp. 380–389.

Laraia, B. A., A. M. Siega-Riz, J. S. Kaufman, and S. J. Jones, "Proximity of Supermarkets Is Positively Associated with Diet Quality Index for Pregnancy," *Preventative Medicine,* Vol. 39, No. 5, 2004, pp. 869–875.

Larson, N., M. Story, and M. Nelson, "Neighborhood Environments: Disparities in Access to Healthy Foods in the U.S," *American Journal of Preventive Medicine,* Vol. 36, No. 1, January 2009, pp. 74–81.

Larson-Meyer, D., and K. Willis, "Vitamin D and Athletes," *Current Sports Medicine Reports,* Vol. 9, No. 4, July–August, 2010, pp. 220–226.

Lau, C., U. Toft, I. Tetens, B. Richelsen, T. Jørgensen, K. Borch-Johnsen, and C. Glümer, "Association Between Dietary Glycemic Index, Glycemic Load, and Body Mass Index in the Inter99 Study: Is Underreporting a Problem?" *American Journal of Clinical Nutrition,* Vol. 84, No. 3, 2006, pp. 641–645.

Laurent, D., K. Schneider, W. Prusaczyk, C. Franklin, S. Vogel, M. Krssak, K. Petersen, H. Goforth, and G. Shulman, "Effects of Caffeine on Muscle Glycogen Utilization and the Neuroendocrine Axis During Exercise," *Clinical Endocrinology Metabolism,* Vol. 85, No. 6, June 2000, pp. 2170–2175.

Lautenschlager, L., and C. Smith, "Beliefs, Knowledge, and Values Held by Inner-City Youth About Gardening, Nutrition, and Cooking," *Agriculture Human Values,* Vol. 24, No. 245-258, 2007.

Lee, H., "The Role of Local Food Availability in Explaining Obesity Risk Among Young School-Aged Children," *Social Science and Medicine*, Vol. 74, No. 8, 2012, pp. 1193–1203.

Levitan, E., A. Wolk, and M. Mittleman, "Consistency with the Dash Diet and Incidence of Heart Failure," *Archives of Internal Medicine,* Vol. 169, No. 9, May 11, 2009, pp. 851–857.

Li, F., P. A. Harmer, B. J. Cardinal, M. Bosworth, A. Acock, D. Johnson-Shelton, and J. M Moore, "Built Environment, Adiposity, and Physical Activity in Adults Aged 50–75," *American Journal of Preventive Medicine,* Vol. 35, No. 1, 2008, pp. 38–46.

Lieberman, H. R., T. Stavinoha, S. McGraw, and L. Sigrist, "Use of Dietary Supplements in U.S. Army Populations," Institute of Medicine Committee on Dietary Supplement Use by Military Personnel meeting, Washington, D.C., February 13, 2007.

Liese, A., M. Schulz, F. Fang, T. Wolever, R. D'Agostino Jr., K. Sparks, and E. Mayer-Davis, "Dietary Glycemic Index and Glycemic Load, Carbohydrate and Fiber Intake, and Measures of Insulin Sensitivity, Secretion, and Adiposity in the Insulin Resistance Atherosclerosis Study," *Diabetes Care,* Vol. 28, No. 12, 2005, pp. 2832–2838.

Lim, S., L. M. Cortina, and V. J. Magley, "Personal and Workgroup Incivility: Impact on Work and Health Outcomes," *Journal of Applied Psychology,* Vol. 93, No. 1, January 2008, pp. 95–107.

Lin, J., E. O'Connor, E. Whitlock, T. Beil, S. Zuber, L. Perdue, D. Plaut, and K. Lutz, "Behavioral Counseling to Promote Physical Activity and a Healthful Diet to Prevent Cardiovascular Disease in Adults: Update of the Evidence for the U.S. Preventive Services Task Force," *Evidence Synthesis,* No. 79, December 2010.

Lineberger, S., and J. Zajicek, "School Gardens: Can a Hands-On Teaching Tool Affect Students' Attitudes and Behaviors Regarding Fruit and Vegetables?" *Hort Technology,* Vol. 10, 2000, pp. 593–597.

Liu, G. C., J. S. Wilson, R. Qi, and J. Ying, "Green Neighborhoods, Food Retail and Childhood Overweight: Differences by Population Density," *American Journal of Health Promotion,* Vol. 21, No. 4 (Supplement), 2007, pp. 317–325.

Liu, S., M. Serdula, D. Williamson, A. Mokdad, and T. Byers, "A Prospective Study of Alcohol Intake and Change in Body Weight Among U.S. Adults," *American Journal of Epidemiology,* Vol. 140, No. 10, November 15, 1994, pp. 912–920.

Liu, S., M. Serdula, S. Janket, N. Cook, H. Sesso, W. Willett, J. Manson, and J. Buring, "A Prospective Study of Fruit and Vegetable Intake and the Risk of Type 2 Diabetes in Women," *Diabetes Care,* Vol. 12, 2004, pp. 2993–2996.

Lloyd, H., M. Green, and P. Rogers, "Mood and Cognitive Performance Effects of Isocaloric Lunches Differing in Fat and Carbohydrate Content," *Physiological Behaviors,* Vol. 56, 1994, pp. 51–57.

Lopez, R. P., "Neighborhood Risk Factors for Obesity," *Obesity,* Vol. 15, No. 8, 2007, pp. 2111–2119.

Louie, J. C. Y., V. M. Flood, D. J. Hector, A. M. Rangan, and T. P. Gill, "Dairy Consumption and Overweight and Obesity: A Systematic Review of Prospective Cohort Studies," *Obesity Reviews,* Vol. 12, 2011, pp. E582–E592.

Maddock, J., "The Relationship Between Obesity and the Prevalence of Fast Food Restaurants: State-Level Analysis," *American Journal of Health Promotion,* Vol. 19, No. 2, 2004, pp. 137–143.

Mann, J., P. Appleby, T. Key, and M. Thorogood, "Dietary Determinants of Ischaemic Heart Disease in Health Conscious Individuals," *Heart,* Vol. 78, No. 5, November, 1997, pp. 450–455.

Mares-Perlman, J., B. Klein, R. Klein, L. Ritter, M. Fisher, and J. Freudenheim, "A Diet History Questionnaire Ranks Nutrient Intakes in Middle-Aged and Older Men and Women Similarly to Multiple Food Records," *Journal of Nutrition* Vol. 123, No. 3, March 1993, pp. 489–501.

Margetts, B., L. Beilin, R. Vandongen, and B. Armstrong, "Vegetarian Diet in Mild Hypertension: A Randomised Controlled Trial," *British Medical Journal,* Vol. 293, No. 6560, December 6, 1986, pp. 1468–1471.

Mayo Clinic, "Ephedra (Ephedra sínica)/ma huang," September 1, 2012. As of October 25, 2013: http://www.mayoclinic.com/health/ephedra/NS_patient-ephedra

Mcaleese, J., and L. Rankin, "Garden-Based Nutrition Education Affects Fruit and Vegetable Consumption in Sixth-Grade Adolescents," *Journal of American Diet Association,* Vol. 107, No. 4, April 2007, pp. 662–665.

McAuley, K., C. Hopkins, K. Smith, R. Mclay, S. Williams, R. Taylor, and J. Mann, "Comparison of High-Fat and High-Protein Diets with a High-Carbohydrate Diet in Insulin-Resistant Obese Women," *Diabetologia,* Vol. 48, No. 1, January 2005, pp. 8–16.

McClain, A., C. Chappuis, S. Nguyen-Rodriguez, A. Yaroch, and D. Spruijt-Metz, "Psychosocial Correlates of Eating Behavior in Children and Adolescents: A Review," *International Journal of Behavior, Nutrition, and Physical Activity,* Vol. 6, No. 54, August 12, 2009.

McGene, J., *Social Fitness and Resilience: A Review of Relevant Constructs, Measures, and Links to Well-Being.* Santa Monica, Calif.: RAND Corporation, RR-108-AF, 2013. As of October 3, 2013: http://www.rand.org/pubs/research_reports/RR108.html

McGinnis, J., J. Gootman, and V. Kraak, *Food Marketing to Children and Youth: Threat Or Opportunity?* Community Food Market: Diets Children Youth, Washington: National Academy Press, 2006.

Meadows, S. O., and L. L. Miller, *Airman and Family Resilience: Lessons from the Scientific Literature*, Santa Monica, Calif.: RAND Corporation, RR-106-AF, forthcoming.

Mehta, N. K., and V. W Chang, "Weight Status and Restaurant Availability a Multilevel Analysis," *American Journal of Preventive Medicine,* Vol. 34, No. 2, 2008, pp. 127–133.

Mendez, M., M. Covas, J. Marrugat, J. Vila, and H. Schröder, "Glycemic Load, Glycemic Index, and Body Mass Index in Spanish Adults," *American Journal of Clinical Nutrition,* Vol. 89, No. 1, 2009, pp. 316–322.

Merten, M., A. Williams, and L. Shriver, "Breakfast Consumption in Adolescence and Young Adulthood: Parental Presence, Community Context, and Obesity," *Journal of American Diet Association,* Vol. 109, No. 8, 2009, pp. 1384–1391.

Michigan Healthy Communities Collaborative, "Welcome to the Online Home of the Nutrition Environment Assessment Tool (NEAT)," undated.

Miller, E. 3rd, T. Erlinger, D. Young, M. Jehn, J. Charleston, D. Rhodes, S. Wasan, and L. Appel, "Results of the Diet, Exercise, and Weight Loss Intervention Trial (Dew-It)," *Hypertension,* Vol. 40, No. 5, November 2002, pp. 612–618.

Milton, J., B. Briche, I. Brown, M. Hickson, C. Robertson, and G. Frost, "Relationship of Glycemic Index with Cardiovascular Risk Factors: Analysis of the National Diet and Nutrition Survey for People Aged 65 and Older," *Public Health Nutrition,* Vol. 10, No. 11, 2007, pp. 1321–1335.

Mirmiran, P., N. Noori, M. Zavareh, and F. Azizi, "Fruit and Vegetable Consumption and Risk Factors for Cardiovascular Disease," *Metabolism,* Vol. 58, No. 4, April 2009, pp. 460–468.

Mission: Readiness, "Too Fat to Fight: Retired Military Leaders Want Junk Food Out of America's Schools" April 8, 2010. As of October 25, 2013: http://cdn.missionreadiness.org/MR_Too_Fat_to_Fight-1.pdf

Mobley, L. R., E. D. Root, E. A. Finkelstein, O. Khavjou, R. P. Farris, and J. C. Will, "Environment, Obesity, and Cardiovascular Disease Risk in Low-Income Women," *American Journal of Preventive Medicine,* Vol. 30, No. 4, 2006, pp. 327–332.

Montain, S. J., C. E. Carvey, and M. B. Stephens, "Nutritional Fitness," *Military Medicine,* Vol. 175, No. 8, 2010, p. 65.

Montain, S. J., H. L. McClung, S. M. McGraw, and M. Ely, " Commercial Caffeinated Products For Military Use: Customer Acceptability," USARIEM TECHNICAL REPORT T12-02, 2012.

Moore, L. V., A. V. Diez Roux, and S. Brines, "Comparing Perception-Based and Geographic Information System (GIS)-Based Characterizations of the Local Food Environment," *Journal of Urban Health: Bulletin of the New York Academy of Medicine,* Vol. 85, No. 2, 2008, p. 11.

Moore, Q., "Nutrition Environment Assessment Tool (NEAT)," Michigan Department of Health, 2005.

Morland, K., S. Wing, and A. V. Diez Roux, "The Contextual Effect of the Local Food Environment on Residents' Diets: The Atherosclerosis Risk in Communities Study," *American Journal of Public Health,* Vol. 92, No. 11, 2002, pp. 1761–1767.

Morland, K., A. V. Diez Roux, and S. Wing, "Supermarkets, Other Food Stores, and Obesity: The Atherosclerosis Risk in Communities Study," *American Journal of Preventive Medicine,* Vol. 30, No. 4, 2006, pp. 333–339.

Morris, J., and S. Zidenberg-Cherr, "Garden-Enhanced Nutrition Curriculum Improves Fourth-Grade School Children's Knowledge of Nutrition and Preferences for Some Vegetables," *Journal of American Diet Association,* Vol. 102, No. 1, January 2002, pp. 91–93.

Morris, J., A. Neustadter, and S. Zidenberg-Cherr, "First-Grade Gardeners More Likely to Taste Vegetables," *California Agriculture*, 2001, pp. 43–46.

Mosdøl, A., D. Witte, G. Frost, M. Marmot, and E. Brunner, "Dietary Glycemic Index and Glycemic Load Are Associated with High-Density-Lipoprotein Cholesterol at Baseline But Not with Increased Risk of Diabetes in the Whitehall Ii Study," *American Journal of Clinical Nutrition,* Vol. 86, No. 4, 2007, pp. 988–994.

Moshfegh, A., J. Goldman, J. Ahuja, D. Rhodes, and R. Lacomb, *What We Eat in American: NHANES 2005–2006*, Washington, D.C.: U.S. Department of Agriculture, 2009.

Mozaffarian, D., T. Hao, E. Rimm, W. Willett, and F. Hu, "Changes in Diet and Lifestyle and Long-Term Weight Gain in Women and Men," *New England Journal of Medicine,* Vol. 364, No. 25, June 23, 2011, pp. 2392–2404.

Mujahid, M. S., A. V. Diez Roux, M. Shen, D. Gowda, B. Sanchez, S. Shea, D. R. Jacobs, and S. A Jackson, "Relation Between Neighborhood Environments and Obesity in the Multi-Ethnic Study of Atherosclerosis," *American Journal of Epidemiology,* Vol. 167, No. 11, 2008, pp. 1349–1357.

Mukamal, K., H. Chung, N. Jenny, L. Kuller, W. Longstreth, Jr., M. Mittleman, G. Burke, M. Cushman, N. Beauchamp, Jr., and D. Siscovick, "Alcohol Use and Risk of Ischemic Stroke Among Older Adults: The Cardiovascular Health Study," *Stroke,* Vol. 36, No. 9, September 2005a, pp. 1830–1834.

Mukamal, K., M. Maclure, J. Muller, and M. Mittleman, "Binge Drinking and Mortality After Acute Myocardial Infarction," *Circulation,* Vol. 112, No. 25, December 20, 2005b, pp. 3839–3845.

Mullen, Admiral M., "On Total Force Fitness in War and Peace," *Military Medicine*, Vol. 175 (Supplement), 2010, pp. 1–2.

Murakami, K., S. Sasaki, H. Okubo, Y. Takahashi, Y. Hosoi, and M. Itabashi, "Dietary Fiber Intake, Dietary Glycemic Index and Load, and Body Mass Index: A Cross-Sectional Study of 3931 Japanese Women Aged 18–20 Years," *European Journal of Clinical Nutrition,* Vol. 61, No. 8, 2007, pp. 986–995.

Myers, J., R. Housemann, and S. Lovegreen, "Organizational Characteristics and Worksite Survey," St. Louis University School of Public Health, 2008.

Nath, S. D., and F. G. Huffman, "Validation of a Semiquantitative Food Frequency Questionnaire to Assess Energy and Macronutrient Intakes of Cuban Americans," *International Journal of Food Sciences and Nutrition,* Vol. 56, No. 5, August 2005, pp. 309–314.

National Cancer Institute, Applied Research: Cancer Control and Population Sciences, "Diet History II," September 3, 2013a. As of October 24, 2013:
http://riskfactor.cancer.gov/dhq2/

———, Applied Research: Cancer Control and Population Sciences, "Diet History Questionnaire Paper-Based Forms," October 18, 2013b. As of October 24, 2013:
http://riskfactor.cancer.gov/DHQ/forms/

National Institutes of Health, "Dietary Supplement Fact Sheet: Vitamin D," Bethesda, Md., June 24, 2011.

———, "Bone Mass Measurements: What the Numbers Mean," Bethesda, Md., January 2012: As of October 28, 2013:
http://www.niams.nih.gov/Health_Info/Bone/

National Institutes of Medicine, *Dietary Reference Intakes for Water, Potassium, Sodium, Chloride, and Sulfate*, National Academies Press, Washington, D.C., 2005. As of October 19, 2013:
http://www.nap.edu/openbook.php?record_id=10925

Nelson, M. C., P. Gordon-Larsen, Y. Song, and B. M Popkin, "Built and Social Environments Associations with Adolescent Overweight and Activity," *American Journal of Preventive Medicine,* Vol. 31, No. 2, 2006, pp. 109–117.

Nicolai, S., L. Kruidenier, B. Bendermacher, M. Prins, and J. Teijink, "Ginkgo Biloba for Intermittent Claudication," *Cochrane Database of Systematic Reviews*, No. 2, 2009.

Nielsen, B., K. Bjørnsbo, I. Tetens, and B. Heitmann, "Dietary Glycemic Index and Glycemic Load in Danish Children in Relation to Body Fatness," *British Journal of Nutrition,* Vol. 94, No. 6, 2005, pp. 992–997.

Niemeier, H. M, H. A. Raynor, E. E. Lloyd-Richardson, M. L. Rogers, and R. R. Wing, "Fast Food Consumption and Breakfast Skipping: Predictors of Weight Gain from Adolescence to Adulthood in a Nationally Representative Sample," *Journal of Adolescent Health,* Vol. 39, 2006, pp. 842–849.

Nordmann, A., A. Nordmann, M. Briel, U. Keller, W. Yancy, Jr., B. Brehm, and H. Bucher, "Effects of Low-Carbohydrate Vs Low-Fat Diets on Weight Loss and Cardiovascular Risk

Factors: A Meta-Analysis of Randomized Controlled Trials," *Archives of Internal Medicine,* Vol. 166, No. 3, 2006, pp. 285–293.

Nowson, C. A., A. Worsley, C. Margerison, M. K. Jorna, A. G. Frame, S. J. Torres, and S. J. Godfrey, "Blood Pressure Response to Dietary Modifications in Free-Living Individuals," *Journal of Nutrition,* Vol. 134, No. 9, September 2004, pp. 2322–2329.

Nowson, C. A. , A. Worsley, C. Margerison, M. K. Jorna, S. J. Godfrey, and A. Booth, "Blood Pressure Change with Weight Loss Is Affected by Diet Type in Men," *American Journal of Clinical Nutr*ition, Vol. 81, No. 5, May 2005, pp. 983–989.

Nowson, C., N. Wattanapenpaiboon, and A. Pachett, "Low-Sodium Dietary Approaches to Stop Hypertension-Type Diet Including Lean Red Meat Lowers Blood Pressure in Postmenopausal Women," *Nutrition Research,* Vol. 29, No. 1, January 2009, pp. 8–18.

O'Brien, S., and C. Shoemaker, "An After-School Gardening Club to Promote Fruit and Vegetable Consumption Among Fourth Grade Students: The Assessment of the Social Cognitive Theory Constructs," *Hort Technology,* Vol. 16, 2006, pp. 24–29.

Ogden, C. L., M. D. Carroll, B. K. Kit, and K. M. Flegal, "Prevalence of Obesity in the United States, 2009–2010," NCHS Data Brief, No. 82, January 2012.

Ohri-Vachaspati, P., and L. C. Leviton, "Measuring Food Environments: A Guide to Available Instruments," *The Science of Health Promotion,* Vol. 24, No. 6, July–August 2010, pp. 410–426.

Oldenburg, B., D. Harris Sallis, and N. Owen, "Checklist of Health Promotion Environments at Worksites (CHEW): Development and Measurement Characteristics," *American Journal of Health Promotion,* Vol. 16, No. 5, May–June 2002, pp. 288–299.

Ortega, R., E. Rodríguez-Rodríguez, A. Aparicio, L. Marín-Arias, and A. López-Sobaler, "Responses to Two Weight-Loss Programs Based on Approximating the Diet to the Ideal: Differences Associated with Increased Cereal Or Vegetable Consumption," *International Journal of Vitamin and Nutritional Research,* Vol. 76, No. 6, 2006, pp. 367–376.

Osler, M., B. Heitmann, L. Gerdes, L. Jørgensen, and M. Schroll, "Dietary Patterns and Mortality in Danish Men and Women: A Prospective Observational Study," *British Journal of Nutrition,* Vol. 85, No. 2, February 2001, pp. 219–225.

Pan, A., Q. Sun, A. M. Bernstein, M. B. Schulze, J. E. Manson, M. J. Stampfer, W. C. Willett, and F. B. Hu, "Red Meat Consumption and Mortality: Results from 2 Prospective Cohort Studies," *Archives of Internal Medicine,* Vol. 172, No. 7, April 9, 2012, pp. 555–563.

Papas, M., A. Alberg, R. Ewing, K. Helzlsouer, T. Gary, and A. Klassen, "The Built Environment and Obesity," *Epidemiologic Reviews,* Vol. 29, 2007, pp. 129–143.

Parikh, A., S. Lipsitz, and S. Natarajan, "Association Between a Dash-Like Diet and Mortality in Adults with Hypertension: Findings From a Population-Based Follow-Up Study," *American Journal of Hypertension,* Vol. 22, No. 4, April 2009, pp. 409–416.

Pearcey, S., and J. De Castro, "Food Intake and Meal Patterns of Weight-Stable and Weight-Gaining Persons," *American Journal of Clinical Nutrition,* Vol. 76, No. 1, 2002, pp. 107–112.

Philippou, E., N. Neary, O. Chaudhri, A. Brynes, A. Dornhorst, A. Leeds, M. Hickson, and G. Frost, "The Effect of Dietary Glycemic Index on Weight Maintenance in Overweight Subjects: A Pilot Study," *Obesity,* Vol. 17, No. 2, February 2009, pp. 396–401.

Pittas, A., S. Roberts, S. Das, C. Gilhooly, E. Saltzman, J. Golden, P. Stark, and A. Greenberg, "The Effects of the Dietary Glycemic Load on Type 2 Diabetes Risk Factors During Weight Loss," *Obesity,* Vol. 14, No. 12, 2006, pp. 2200–2209.

Poortinga, W., "Perceptions of the Environment, Physical Activity, and Obesity," *Social Science & Medicine,* Vol. 63, No. 11, 2006, pp. 2835–2846.

Popkin, B., K. D'anci, and I. Rosenberg, "Water, Hydration, and Health," *Nutrition Review,* Vol. 68, No. 8, 2010, pp. 439–458.

Poston, S., C. Shoemaker, and D. Dzewaltowski, "A Comparison of a Gardening and Nutrition Program with a Standard Nutrition Program in an Out-of-School Setting," *Hort Technology,* Vol. 15, 2005, pp. 463–467.

Powell, L. M., M. C. Auld, F. J. Chaloupka, P. M. O'Malley, and L. D Johnston, "Associations Between Access to Food Stores and Adolescent Body Mass Index," *American Journal of Preventive Medicine,* Vol. 33, No. 4 (Supplement), 2007, pp. S301–S307.

Prentice, R., B. Caan, R. Chlebowski, et al., "Low-Fat Dietary Pattern and Risk of Invasive Breast Cancer: The Women's Health Initiative Randomized Controlled Dietary Modification Trial," *Journal of American Medical Association,* Vol. 295, 2006, pp. 629–642.

Puder, J., and S. Munsch, "Psychological Correlates of Childhood Obesity," *International Journal of Obesity,* Vol. 34 (Supplement 2), December 2010, pp. S37–S43.

Purslow, L., M. Sandhu, N. Forouhi, E. Young, R. Luben, A. Welch, K. Khaw, S. Bingham, and N. Wareham, "Energy Intake at Breakfast and Weight Change: Prospective Study of 6,764 Middle-Aged Men and Women," *American Journal of Epidemiology,* Vol. 167, No. 2, 2008, pp. 188–1982.

Raatz, S., C. Torkelson, J. Redmon, K. Reck, C. Kwong, J. Swanson, C. Liu, W. Thomas, and J. Bantle, "Reduced Glycemic Index and Glycemic Load Diets Do Not Increase the Effects of Energy Restriction on Weight Loss and Insulin Sensitivity in Obese Men and Women," *Journal of Nutrition,* Vol. 135, No. 10, 2005, pp. 2387–2391.

Radhika, G., V. Sudha, S. R. Mohan, A. Ganesan, and V. Mohan, "Association of Fruit and Vegetable Intake with Cardiovascular Risk Factors in Urban South Indians," *British Journal of Nutrition,* Vol. 99, No. 2, 2008, pp. 398–405.

Robson, S., *Physical Fitness and Resilience: A Review of Relevant Constructs, Measures, and Links to Well-Being.* Santa Monica, Calif.: RAND Corporation, RR-104-AF, 2013. As of October 3, 2013:
http://www.rand.org/pubs/research_reports/RR104.html

———, *Psychological Fitness and Resilience: A Review of Relevant Constructs, Measures, and Links to Well-Being.* Santa Monica, Calif.: RAND Corporation, RR-102-AF, 2014. As of March 11, 2014:
http://www.rand.org/pubs/research_reports/RR102.html

Robson, S., and N. Salcedo, *Behavioral Fitness and Resilience: A Review of Relevant Constructs, Measures, and Links to Well-Being.* Santa Monica, Calif.: RAND Corporation, RR-103-AF, forthcoming.

Roderick, P., V. Ruddock, P. Hunt, and G. Miller, "A Randomized Trial to Evaluate the Effectiveness of Dietary Advice by Practice Nurses in Lowering Diet-Related Coronary Heart Disease Risk," *British Journal of General Practice,* Vol. 47, 1997, pp. 7–12.

Rodriguez, N., N. Di Marco, and S. Langley, "American College of Sports Medicine Position Stand: Nutrition and Athletic Performance," *American Dietetic Association; Dietitians of Canada; American College of Sports Medicine,* Vol. 41, No. 3, March 2009, pp. 709–731.

Rofey, D., R. Kolko, A. Iosif, J. Silk, J. Bost, W. Feng, E. Szigethy, R. Noll, N. Ryan, and R. Dahl, "A Longitudinal Study of Childhood Depression and Anxiety in Relation to Weight Gain," *Child Psychiatry and Human Development,* Vol. 40, 2009, pp. 517–526.

Rogers, P. J., and A. J. Hill, "Breakdown of Dietary Restraint Following Mere Exposure to Food Stimuli: Interrelationships Between Restraint, Hunger, Salivation, and Food Intake," *Addictive Behaviors,* Vol. 14, No. 4, 1989, pp. 387–397.

Rolls, B. J., "The Relationship Between Dietary Energy Density and Energy Intake," *Physiology & Behavior*, Vol. 97, No. 5, July 2009, pp. 609–615

Rolls, B., L. Roe, A. Beach, and P. Kris-Etherton, "Provision of Foods Differing in Energy Density Affects Long-Term Weight Loss," *Obesity Research,* Vol. 13, No. 6, 2005, pp. 1052–1060.

Rose, D., and R. Richards, "Food Store Access and Household Fruit and Vegetable Use Among Participants in the US Food Stamp Program," *Public Health Nutrition,* Vol. 7, No. 8, 2004, pp. 1081–1088.

Rosenheck, R., "Fast Food Consumption and Increased Caloric Intake: A Systematic Review of a Trajectory Towards Weight Gain and Obesity Risk," *Obesity Review,* Vol. 9, No. 6, 2008, pp. 535–547.

Rouse, I., L. Beilin, B. Armstrong, and R. Vandongen, "Blood-Pressure-Lowering Effect of a Vegetarian Diet: Controlled Trial in Normotensive Subjects," *Lancet,* Vol. 1, No. 8314-5, 1983, pp. 5–10.

Sacerdote, C., L. Fiorini, R. Rosato, M. Audenino, M. Valpreda, and P. Vineis, "Randomized Controlled Trial: Effect of Nutritional Counseling in General Practice," *International Journal of Epidemiology,* Vol. 35, 2006, pp. 409–415.

Sacks, F., L. Svetkey, W. Vollmer, L. Appel, G. Bray, D. Harsha, E. Obarzanek, P. Conlin, E. Miller, 3rd, D. Simons-Morton, N. Karanja, and P. Lin, "Effects on Blood Pressure of Reduced Dietary Sodium and the Dietary Approaches to Stop Hypertension (Dash) Diet," *New England Journal of Medicine,* Vol. 344, No. 1, January 4, 2001, pp. 3–10.

Sacks, F., G. Bray, V. Carey, S. Smith, D. Ryan, S. Anton, K. Mcmanus, C. Champagne, L. Bishop, N. Laranjo, M. Leboff, J. Rood, L. De Jonge, F. Greenway, C. Loria, E. Obarzanek, and D. Williamson, "Comparison of Weight-Loss Diets with Different Compositions of Fat, Protein, and Carbohydrates," *New England Journal of Medicine,* Vol. 360, No. 9, 2009, pp. 859–873.

Sadiq-Butt, M., and M. Sultan, "Coffee and Its Consumption: Benefits and Risks," *Critical Review of Food Science and Nutrition,* Vol. 51, No. 4, April 2011, pp. 363–373.

Saha, S., U. Gerdtham, and P. Johansson, "Economic Evaluation of Lifestyle Interventions for Preventing Diabetes and Cardiovascular Diseases," *International Journal of Environmental Research and Public Health,* Vol. 7, No. 8, August 2010, pp. 3150–3195.

Sahyoun, N., A. Anderson, F. Tylavsky, J. Lee, D. Sellmeyer, and T. Harris, "Health, Aging, and Body Composition Study: Dietary Glycemic Index and Glycemic Load and the Risk of Type 2 Diabetes in Older Adults," *American Journal of Clinical Nutrition,* Vol. 87, No. 1, 2008, pp. 126–131.

Sammel, M., J. Grisso, E. Freeman, L. Hollander, L. Liu, S. Liu, D. Nelson, and M. Battistini, "Weight Gain Among Women in the Late Reproductive Years," *Family Practice,* Vol. 20, No. 4, August 2003, pp. 401–409.

Samuels and Associates, "Neighborhood Food and Beverage Environment Assessment Tool," 2006. As of November 12, 2013:
http://www.samuelsandassociates.com

Samuels and Associates, "Improving Health by Informing Environmental and Policy Change," 2011.

Schulz, M., A. Liese, F. Fang, T. Gilliard, and A. Karter, "Is the Association Between Dietary Glycemic Index and Type 2 Diabetes Modified by Waist Circumference?" *Diabetes Care,* Vol. 29, No. 5, May 2006, pp. 1102–1104.

Schulze, M., K. Hoffmann, A. Kroke, and H. Boeing, "Risk of Hypertension Among Women in the Epic-Potsdam Study: Comparison of Relative Risk Estimates for Exploratory and Hypothesis-Oriented Dietary Patterns," *American Journal of Epidemiology,* Vol. 158, No. 4, August 15, 2003, pp. 365–373.

Schulze, M., S. Liu, E. Rimm, J. Manson, W. Willett, and F. Hu, "Glycemic Index, Glycemic Load, and Dietary Fiber Intake and Incidence of Type 2 Diabetes in Younger and Middle-Aged Women," *American Journal of Clinical Nutrition,* Vol. 80, No. 2, 2004, pp. 348–356.

Sciarrone, S., M. Strahan, L. Beilin, V. Burke, P. Rogers, and I. Rouse, "Ambulatory Blood Pressure and Heart Rate Responses to Vegetarian Meals," *Journal of Hypertension,* Vol. 11, No. 3, 1993, pp. 277–285.

Shaikh, A., A. Yaroch, L. Nebeling, M. Yeh, and K. Resnicow, "Psychosocial Predictors of Fruit and Vegetable Consumption in Adults a Review of the Literature," *American Journal Preview Medicine,* Vol. 34, No. 6, June 2008, pp. 535–543.

Shatenstein, B., and P. Ghadirian, "Influences on Diet, Health Behaviours and Their Outcome in Select Ethnocultural and Religious Groups," *Nutrition,* Vol. 14, 1998, pp. 223–230.

Sherwood, N., R. Jeffery, S. French, P. Hannan, and D. Murray, "Predictors of Weight Gain in the Pound of Prevention Study," *International Journal of Obesity Related and Metabolic Disorders,* Vol. 24, No. 4, April 2000, pp. 395–403.

Shih, R. A., S. O. Meadows, and M. T. Martin, *Medical Fitness and Resilience: A Review of Relevant Constructs, Measures, and Links to Well-Being.* Santa Monica, Calif.: RAND Corporation, RR-107-AF, 2013. As of October 3, 2013: http://www.rand.org/pubs/research_reports/RR107.html

Shih, R. A., S. O. Meadows, J. M. Mendeloff, and K. Bowling, *Environmental Fitness and Resilience: A Review of Relevant Constructs, Measures, and Links to Well-Being.* Santa Monica, Calif.: RAND Corporation, RR-101-AF, forthcoming.

Shimazu, T., S. Kuriyama, A. Hozawa, K. Ohmori, Y. Sato, N. Nakaya, Y. Nishino, Y. Tsubono, and I. Tsuji, "Dietary Patterns and Cardiovascular Disease Mortality in Japan: A Prospective Cohort Study," *International Journal of Epidemiology,* Vol. 36, No. 3, June 2007, pp. 600–609.

Shimotsu, S., S. French, A. Gerlach, and P. Hannan, "Worksite Environment Physical Activity and Healthy Food Choices: Measurement of the Worksite Food and Physical Activity

Environment at Four Metropolitan Bus Garages," *International Journal of Behavior, Nutrition, and Physical Activity,* Vol. 4, No. 17, May 11, 2007.

Sichieri, R., A. Moura, V. Genelhu, F. Hu, and W. Willett, "An 18-Mo Randomized Trial of a Low-Glycemic-Index Diet and Weight Change in Brazilian Women," *American Journal of Clinical Nutrition,* Vol. 86, No. 3, 2007, pp. 707–713.

Simmons, D., A. Mckenzie, S. Eaton, N. Cox, M. A. Khan, J. Shaw, and P. Zimmet, "Choice and Availability of Takeaway and Restaurant Food Is Not Related to the Prevalence of Adult Obesity in Rural Communities in Australia," *International Journal of Obesity,* Vol. 29, No. 6, 2005, pp. 703–710.

Singman, H., S. Berman, C. Cowell, E. Maslansky, and M. Archer, "The Anti-Coronary Club: 1957 to 1972," *American Journal of Clinical Nutrition,* Vol. 33, No. 6, June, 1980, pp. 1183–1191.

Slavin, J. L., "Position of the American Dietetic Association: Health Implications of Dietary Fiber," *Journal of American Diet Association,* Vol. 108, No. 10, October 2008, pp. 1716–1731.

Sloth, B., I. Krog-Mikkelsen, A. Flint, I. Tetens, I. Björck, S. Vinoy, H. Elmståhl, A. Astrup, V. Lang, and A. Raben, "No Difference in Body Weight Decrease Between a Low-Glycemic-Index and a High-Glycemic-Index Diet But Reduced LDL Cholesterol After 10-Wk Ad Libitum Intake of the Low-Glycemic-Index Diet," *American Journal of Clinical Nutrition,* Vol. 80, No. 2, 2004, pp. 337–347.

Snyder, L. B., "Health Communication Campaigns and Their Impact on Behavior," *Journal of Nutrition, Education, and Behavior,* Vol. 39, No. 2 (Supplement), March–April 2007, pp. S32–S40.

Spencer, E., P. Appleby, G. Davey, and T. Key, "Diet and Body Mass Index in 38000 Epic-Oxford Meat-Eaters, Fish-Eaters, Vegetarians and Vegans," *International Journal of Obesity and Related Metabolic Disorders,* Vol. 27, No. 6, 2003, pp. 728–734.

Spiegel, T. A., J. M. Kaplan, A. Tomassini, and E. Stellar, "Bite Size, Ingestion Rate, and Meal Size in Lean and Obese Women," *Appetite,* Vol. 21, No. 2, 1993, pp. 131–145

Stefanick, M., S. Mackey, M. Sheehan, N. Ellsworth, W. Haskell, and P. Wood, "Effects of Diet and Exercise in Men and Postmenopausal Women with Low Levels of HDL Cholesterol and High Levels of LDL Cholesterol," *New England Journal of Medicine,* Vol. 339, 1998, pp. 12–20.

Steptoe, A., E. Gibson, R. Vuononvirta, E. Williams, M. Hamer, J. Rycroft, J. Erusalimsky, and J. Wardle, "The Effects of Tea on Psychophysiological Stress Responsivity and Post-Stress

Recovery: A Randomised Double-Blind Trial," *Psychopharmacology (Berl),* Vol. 190, No. 1, January 2007, pp. 81–89.

Stevens, J., K. Ahn, D. Houston, L. Steffan, and D. Couper, "Dietary Fiber Intake and Glycemic Index and Incidence of Diabetes in African-American and White Adults: The Aric Study," *Diabetes Care,* Vol. 25, No. 10, 2002, pp. 1715–1721.

Stokols, D., "Establishing and Maintaining Healthy Environments," *American Psychologist,* Vol. 47, No., 1, 1992, pp. 6–22.

Sturm, R., and A. Datar, "Body Mass Index in Elementary School Children, Metropolitan Area Food Prices and Food Outlet Density," *Public Health,* Vol. 119, No. 12, 2005, pp. 1059–1068.

Subar, A., F. Thompson, V. Kipnis, D. Midthune, P. Hurwitz, S. Mcnutt, A. McIntosh, and S. Rosenfeld, "Comparative Validation of the Block, Willett, and National Cancer Institute Food Frequency Questionnaires: The Eating at America's Table Study," *American Journal of Epidemiology,* Vol. 154, No. 12, December 15, 2001, pp. 1089–1099.

Sun, S., and M. Empie, "Lack of Findings for the Association Between Obesity Risk and Usual Sugar-Sweetened Beverage Consumption in Adults—A Primary Analysis of Databases of Csfii-1989-1991, Csfii-1994-1998, Nhanes Iii, and Combined Nhanes 1999-2002," *Food and Chemical Toxicology,* Vol. 45, No. 8, August 2007, pp. 1523–1536.

Sydenham, E., A. D. Dangour, and W. S. Lim, "Omega 3 Fatty Acid for the Prevention of Cognitive Decline and Dementia," *Cochrane Database Systematic Reviews*, Vol. 13, No. 6, 2012.

Tanihara, S., T. Imatoh, M. Miyazaki, A. Babazono, Y. Momose, M. Baba, Y. Uryu, and H. Une, "Retrospective Longitudinal Study on the Relationship Between 8-Year Weight Change and Current Eating Speed," *Appetite,* Vol. 57, No. 1, August 2011, pp. 179–183.

Tanofsky-Kraff, M., M. D. Marcus, S. Z. Yanovski, and J. A. Yanovski, "Loss of Control Eating Disorder in Children Age 12y and Younger: Proposed Research Criteria," *Eating Behavior,* Vol. 9, No. 3, August 2008, pp. 360–365.

Tanumihardjo, S., A. Valentine, Z. Zhang, L. Whigham, H. Lai, and R. Atkinson, "Strategies to Increase Vegetable Or Reduce Energy and Fat Intake Induce Weight Loss in Adults," *Experimental Biology and Medicine,* Vol. 234, No. 5, 2009, pp. 542–552.

Tarnopolsky, M., "Caffeine and Creatine Use in Sport," *Annual Nutrition Metabolism,* Vol. 57, 2010 (Supplement 2), pp. 1–8.

Tay, J., G. Brinkworth, M. Noakes, J. Keogh, and P. Clifton, "Metabolic Effects of Weight Loss on a Very-Low-Carbohydrate Diet Compared with an Isocaloric High-Carbohydrate Diet in

Abdominally Obese Subjects," *Journal of American College of Cardiology,* Vol. 51, No. 1, January 2008, pp. 59–67.

Tinker, L., D. Bonds, K. Margolis, J. Manson, B. Howard, J. Larson, M. Perri, S. Beresford, J. Robinson, B. Rodríguez, M. Safford, N. Wenger, V. Stevens, and L. Parker, "Low-Fat Dietary Pattern and Risk of Treated Diabetes Mellitus in Postmenopausal Women: The Women's Health Initiative Randomized Controlled Dietary Modification Trial," *Archives of Internal Medicine,* Vol. 168, 2008, pp. 1500–1511.

Tolstrup, J., J. Halkjaer, B. Heitmann, A. Tjønneland, K. Overvad, T. Sørensen, and M. Grønbaek, "Alcohol Drinking Frequency in Relation to Subsequent Changes in Waist Circumference," *American Journal of Clinical Nutrition,* Vol. 87, No. 4, 2008, pp. 957–963.

Tucker, K., J. Hallfrisch, N. Qiao, D. Muller, R. Andres, and J. Fleg, "The Combination of High Fruit and Vegetable and Low Saturated Fat Intakes Is More Protective Against Mortality in Aging Men Than Is Either Alone: The Baltimore Longitudinal Study of Aging," *Journal of Nutrition,* Vol. 135, No. 3, March 2005, pp. 556–561.

U.S. Army Public Health Command, "Dietary Supplements," undated. As of November 13, 2013:
http://phc.amedd.army.mil/topics/healthyliving/n/Pages/DietarySupplements.aspx

U.S. Department of Agriculture, "What We Eat in America," November 13, 2013. As of November 13, 2013:
http://www.ars.usda.gov/Services/docs.htm?docid=13793

U.S. Department of Agriculture and U.S. Department of Health and Human Services, *The Dietary Guidelines for Americans*, Washington, D.C.: U.S. Government Printing office, 2010.

U.S. Department of Health and Human Services, *What We Eat*, Washington, D.C., 2004.

U.S. Food and Drug Administration, Dietary Supplements Guidance Documents and Regulatory Information, August 19, 2013.

Van Der Horst, K., A. Oenema, I. Ferreira, W. Wendel-Vos, K. Giskes, F. Van Lenthe, and J. Brug, "A Systematic Review of Environmental Correlates of Obesity-Related Dietary Behaviors in Youth," *Health and Education Research,* Vol. 22, No. 2, 2007, pp. 203–226.

Van Staveren, W. A., and M. C. Ocké, *Estimation of Dietary Intake,* 9th ed., Vol. 2, *Present Knowledge in Nutrition*, 2006.

Villegas, R., S. Liu, Y. Gao, G. Yang, H. Li, W. Zheng, and X. Shu, "Prospective Study of Dietary Carbohydrates, Glycemic Index, Glycemic Load, and Incidence of Type 2 Diabetes Mellitus in Middle-Aged Chinese Women," *Archives of Internal Medicine,* Vol. 167, No. 21, 2007, pp. 2310–2316.

Vioque, J., T. Weinbrenner, A. Castelló, L. Asensio, and M. Garcia De La Hera, "Intake of Fruits and Vegetables in Relation to 10-Year Weight Gain Among Spanish Adults," *Obesity,* Vol. 16, No. 3, 2008, pp. 664–670.

Volkow, N. D., "This Is Your Brain on Food," *Scientific American,* Vol. 297, No. 3, September 2007, pp. 84–85.

Walsh, R., "Lifestyle and Mental Health," *American Psychologist*, January 17, 2011.

Wang, L., S. Liu, J. Manson, J. Gaziano, J. Buring, and H. Sesso, "The Consumption of Lycopene and Tomato-Based Food Products Is Not Associated with the Risk of Type 2 Diabetes in Women," *Journal of Nutrition,* Vol. 136, No. 3, 2006, pp. 620–625.

Wang, M. C., S. Kim, A. A. Gonzalez, K. E. Macleod, and M. A. Winkleby, "Socioeconomic and Food-Related Physical Characteristics of the Neighbourhood Environment Are Associated with Body Mass Index," *Journal of Epidemiology and Community Health,* Vol. 61, No. 6, 2007, pp. 491–498.

Wang, Y., W. Yancy, Jr., D. Yu, C. Champagne, L. Appel, and P. Lin, "The Relationship Between Dietary Protein Intake and Blood Pressure: Results from the Premier Study," *Journal of Human Hypertension,* Vol. 22, No. 11, November 2008, pp. 745–754.

Wannamethee, S., and A. Shaper, "Alcohol, Body Weight, and Weight Gain in Middle-Aged Men," *American Journal of Clinical Nutrition,* Vol. 77, No. 5, May 2003, pp. 1312–1317.

Wannamethee, S., A. Field, G. Colditz, and E. Rimm, "Alcohol Intake and 8-Year Weight Gain in Women: A Prospective Study," *Obesity Research,* Vol. 12, No. 9, September 2004, pp. 1386–1396.

Wansink, B., "From Mindless Eating to Mindlessly Eating Better," *Physiology and Behavior,* Vol. 100, 2010, pp. 454–463.

WCRF/AICR—*See* World Cancer Research Fund/American Institute for Cancer Research.

Wells, A., and N. Read, "Influences of Fat, Energy, and Time of Day on Mood and Performance," *Physiological Behaviors,* Vol. 59, 1996, pp. 1069–1076.

Willett, W., and E. Lenart, *Nutritional Epidemiology, Reproducibility and Validity of Food Frequency Questionnaires*, Oxford University Press, 1998.

Wolfe, A., C. Arroyo, S. Tedders, Y. Li, Q. Dai, and J. Zhang, "Dietary Protein and Protein-Rich Food in Relation to Severely Depressed Mood: A 10 Year Follow-Up of a National Cohort," *Progress in Neuro-Psychopharmacology & Biological Psychiatry,* Vol. 35, No. 1, January 15, 2011, pp. 232–238.

World Cancer Research Fund and American Institute for Cancer Research, *Food, Nutrition, Physical Activity, and the Prevention of Cancer: A Global Perspective*, Washington, D.C.: World Cancer Research Fund, 2007.

Wrigley, N., D. Warm, and B. Margetts, "Deprivation, Diet and Food Retail Access: Findings From the Leeds 'Food Deserts' Study," *Environmental Planning* Vol. 35, 2003, pp. 151–188.

Yao, M., Roberts, SB, "Dietary energy density and weight regulation," *Nutrition Reviews,* Vol. 59, 2001, pp. 247-58.

Yeung, D., and M. T. Martin, *Spiritual Fitness and Resilience: A Review of Relevant Constructs, Measures, and Links to Well-Being.* Santa Monica, Calif.: RAND Corporation, RR-100-AF, 2013. As of October 3, 2013:
http://www.rand.org/pubs/research_reports/RR100.html

Xu, F., X. Yin, and S. Tong, "Association Between Excess Bodyweight and Intake of Red Meat and Vegetables Among Urban and Rural Adult Chinese in Nanjing, China," *Asian Pacific Journal of Public Health,* Vol. 19, No. 3, 2007, pp. 3–9.